Daily
Inspiration
for Everyday
Women

A collection of 365 inspirational quotes

Published 2024

Published 2020 by **FiNGER**PRINT!
An imprint of Prakash Books India Pvt. Ltd

113/A, Darya Ganj,
New Delhi-110 002
Email: info@prakashbooks.com/sales@prakashbooks.com

Fingerprint Publishing
@FingerprintP
@fingerprintpublishingbooks
www.fingerprintpublishing.com

DAILY INSPIRATION FOR EVERYDAY WOMEN

ISBN: 978 93 9018 349 4

Daily
Inspiration
for Everyday
Women

A collection of 365 inspirational quotes

Napoleon Hill
Judith Williamson

FiNGERPRINT!

Introduction

Are you serious about success? If so, use this inspirational calendar to serve and remind you daily of your personal commitment to achieve your goals and lifelong purpose.

Designed for women, this inspirational tool enables you to focus on one or two of Dr. Hill's Success Principles per month. Brief descriptions of the 17 success principles align with the daily quotations.

Use this perpetual calendar to jumpstart your journey. As you set short-term and long-term goals for yourself, you will begin to see why many people turn to Dr. Hill for guidance and reassurance as they begin their personal quest toward success.

Good thoughts produce good outcomes. What you think about, you become. Think on these quotations daily and set your sights on success. You will be surprised at how much you can achieve when you fine-tune your focus and ready your aim.

Be your very best always.

Judy Williamson

Definiteness
of Purpose

Definiteness of Purpose is the starting point of all achievement. All individual achievement begins with the adoption of a definite major purpose and a specific plan for its attainment. Without a purpose and a plan, people drift aimlessly throughout life. Lack of Definiteness of Purpose is the greatest stumbling block to 98 out of every 100 persons because they never really define their goals and start toward them with Definiteness of Purpose. Ideas form the foundation of all fortunes and the starting point of all inventions. Once a student learns how to harness the power of his mind and then how to organize the knowledge, he begins to keep his mind on the things he wants and off the things he does not want.

Obtaining a law degree and becoming a lawyer has inspired me to have persistence, personal initiative and concentrated effort.

—Christina Chia

JANUARY 1

Everyone has inside him a piece of good news.
The good news is that you don't yet realize
how great you can be! How much you can
love! What you can accomplish! And what your
potential is!

— *Anne Frank*

The starting point of all personal achievement is
the adoption of a Definite Major Purpose and a
definite plan for its attainment.

— *Napoleon Hill*

JANUARY 2

A great goal in life is the only fortune
worth finding.

— *Jacqueline Kennedy Onassis*

Definiteness of Purpose develops: self-reliance,
personal initiative, imagination, enthusiasm,
self-discipline, and concentration of effort.

— *Napoleon Hill*

JANUARY 3

Let me listen to me and not to them.

— Gertrude Stein

Definiteness of Purpose encourages you to
specialize in success.

— Napoleon Hill

JANUARY 4

Don't let people tell you who you are.

— Diane Sawyer

Definiteness of Purpose encourages budgeting
of time and money so efforts remain focused on
attaining your Definite Major Purpose.

— Napoleon Hill

JANUARY 5

All of us can take steps—no matter how small
and insignificant at the start—in the direction
we want to go.

— *Marsha Sinetar*

Definiteness of Purpose alerts the mind to
opportunities and gives courage for action.

— *Napoleon Hill*

JANUARY 6

If you don't have a dream, how can you
have a dream come true?

— *Faye LaPointe*

Definiteness of Purpose helps develop the
capacity to reach decisions.

— *Napoleon Hill*

JANUARY 7

A year from now you may wish you had
started today.

— Karen Lamb

Definiteness of Purpose inspires the
cooperation of others.

— Napoleon Hill

JANUARY 8

Unfulfilled desires are the dangerous forces.

— Sarah Tarleton Colvin

Definiteness of Purpose prepares the
mind for faith.

— Napoleon Hill

JANUARY 9

I am not afraid . . . I was born to do this.

— Joan of Arc

Definiteness of Purpose provides a
success consciousness.

— Napoleon Hill

JANUARY 10

We conceive children and we conceive projects.

— Julia Cameron

All individual achievements are the result of a
motive or a combination of motives. There are
nine basic motives inspiring all voluntary action.

— Napoleon Hill

JANUARY 11

Maturity is achieved when you understand that
one has to decide.

— *Angela B. McBride*

Motive One:
—the emotion of love (greatest of all motives).

— *Napoleon Hill*

JANUARY 12

Never confuse knowledge with wisdom.
One helps you earn a living, the other
helps you build a life.

— *Sandra Carey*

Motive Two:
—the emotion of sex.

— *Napoleon Hill*

JANUARY 13

The most important thing is not what destiny
does to us, but what we do with it.

— *Florence Nightingale*

Motive Three:
—the desire for material gain.

— *Napoleon Hill*

JANUARY 14

I want to do it because I want to do it.
Women must try to do things as men have tried.
When they fail, their failure must be but
a challenge to others.

— *Amelia Earhart*

Motive Four:
—the desire for self-preservation.

— *Napoleon Hill*

JANUARY 15

This is happiness; to be dissolved into
something complete and great.

— Willa Cather

Motive Five:
—the desire for freedom of body and mind.

— Napoleon Hill

JANUARY 16

How wrong it is for woman to expect the man
to build the world she wants, rather than to set
out to create it for herself.

— Anaïs Nin

Motive Six:
—the desire for self-expression and recognition.

— Napoleon Hill

JANUARY 17

Figuring out who you are is the whole point of
the human experience.

— Anna Quindlen

Motive Seven:
—the desire for life after death.

— Napoleon Hill

JANUARY 18

Action is the antidote to despair.

— Joan Baez

Motive Eight:
—the desire for revenge.

— Napoleon Hill

January 19

My will shall shape my future. Whether I fail or
succeed shall be no man's doing but my own.
I am the force; I can clear any obstacle before
me or I can be lost in the maze. My choice; my
responsibility; win or lose, only I hold the key to
my destiny.

— *Elaine Maxwell*

Motive Nine:
—the emotion of fear.

— *Napoleon Hill*

January 20

It is only the first step that is difficult.

— *Marie De Vichy-Chaconne*

Any dominating idea, plan or purpose held in
the mind through repetition of thought and
emotionalized with a burning desire for its
realization, is taken over by the subconscious
mind and acted upon through whatever natural
and logical means may be available.

— *Napoleon Hill*

JANUARY 21

If you doubt you can accomplish something,
then you can't accomplish it. You have to have
confidence in your ability, and then be tough
enough to follow through.

— Rosalynn Carter

Conscious Mind
- reasoning/thinking
  faculty
- deliberates, analyzes
- selects Definite
  Major Purpose
- guardian of
  subconscious

Subconscious Mind
- natural,
  uncultivated mind
  responds
  instinctively to
  emotion
- develops the power
  of will

— Napoleon Hill

JANUARY 22

One ship drives east and another
drives west
    With the selfsame winds that blow.
'Tis the set of the sails
And not the gales
    Which tells us the way to go.

— Ella Wheeler Wilcox

Any dominating desire, plan or purpose which is
backed by faith is taken over by
the subconscious mind.

— Napoleon Hill

JANUARY 23

Many persons have a wrong idea about what
constitutes true happiness. It is not attained
through self-gratification, but through fidelity to
a worthy purpose.

— Helen Keller

Creative genius lies within the power of
the subconscious mind.

— Napoleon Hill

JANUARY 24

One could always point to a time, a choice, an
act that set the tone for a life and changed a
personal destiny.

— Carol O'Connell

The nine factors responsible for developing
creative genius are: Definiteness of Purpose,
Applied Faith, Enthusiasm, Imagination,
Motive, Personal Initiative, Habit of Going the
Extra Mile, Master Mind Alliance, and Positive
Mental Attitude.

— Napoleon Hill

January 25

Since we are capable of change and
modifications, the future will be in many ways
only as good as we have the courage to make it.

— June Tapp

The power of thought is the only thing
over which any human being has complete,
unquestionable control.

— Napoleon Hill

January 26

You were born God's original. Try not to
become someone's copy.

— Marian Wright Edelman

The subconscious mind appears to be the only
doorway of individual approach to Infinite
Intelligence, and it is capable of being influenced
by the individual.

— Napoleon Hill

JANUARY 27

For what is done or learned by one class of
women becomes, by virtue of their common
womanhood, the property of all women.

— *Elizabeth Blackwell*

Every brain is both a broadcasting station and
a receiving set for the vibrations of thought—a
fact which explains the importance of moving
with Definiteness of Purpose instead of drifting
along in life—since the brain may be so charged
with Definiteness of Purpose that it will begin to
attract the physical appearance of that purpose.

— *Napoleon Hill*

JANUARY 28

The thing women have got to learn is that
nobody gives you power. You just take it.

— *Roseanne Barr*

Nothing can be achieved unless one is willing to
give something in return.

— *Napoleon Hill*

JANUARY 29

All my life I've wanted to be somebody, but
I see now I should have been more specific.

— *Jane Wagner*

Write out a clear, concise plan by which you
intend to achieve your definite major purpose.
Keep this plan to yourself, except for members
of your Master Mind Alliance.

— *Napoleon Hill*

JANUARY 30

Failing to plan is planning to fail.

— *Effie Jones*

Keep your mind on the things you want and off
the things you do not want.

— *Napoleon Hill*

JANUARY 31

We are weaving the future on the loom of today.
— *Grace Dawson*

Remember: Your only limitation is that which
you set up in your own mind by your neglect in
keeping your mental attitude positive.
— *Napoleon Hill*

Master Mind Alliance

The Master Mind Alliance principle consists of an alliance of two or more minds working together in perfect harmony for the attainment of a definite objective. Success does not come without the cooperation of others. The Master Mind Alliance principle is a practical medium through which you may appropriate and use the full benefits of the experience, training, education, specialized knowledge, and native intelligence of others as completely as if it were your own. An active alliance of two or more minds, in a spirit of perfect harmony for the attainment of a common objective, stimulates each mind to a higher degree of courage than that ordinarily experienced, and paves the way for the state of mind known as Faith.

In collegiate Women's Basketball, each team is an organized Master Mind unit unique to itself. It is a requirement of each player to know intuitively what the other players are thinking. In this manner, you maintain the winning edge.

— *Kelley Watts*

FEBRUARY 1

If you don't look out for others, who will
look out for you?

— *Whoopi Goldberg*

The Master Mind principle consists of an
alliance of two or more minds working in
perfect harmony for the attainment of a
definite objective.

— *Napoleon Hill*

FEBRUARY 2

If you have knowledge, let others light
their candles at it.

— *Margaret Fuller*

The Master Mind principle is a practical medium
through which you may appropriate and use the
full benefits of the experience, the training, the
education, the specialized knowledge and native
intelligence of other people, as completely as if
they were your own.

— *Napoleon Hill*

FEBRUARY 3

Never doubt that a small group of thoughtful,
committed people can change the world;
indeed it is the only thing that ever has.

—Margaret Mead

An active alliance of two or more minds in a
spirit of perfect harmony for the attainment of
a common objective, stimulates each mind to
a higher degree of courage than that ordinarily
experienced, and paves the way for that state of
mind known as faith.

— Napoleon Hill

FEBRUARY 4

What is unity, so it is understood, is two
diverse things made one.

— Saint Theresa

Once a Master Mind Alliance is formed, the
group as a whole must become and
remain active.

— Napoleon Hill

FEBRUARY 5

The ones that give, get back in kind.

— *Pam Durban*

The group must move on a definite plan,
at a definite time, toward a definite
common objective.

— *Napoleon Hill*

FEBRUARY 6

Women now know that, besides hard work
and lots of skill, the move to the top requires a
supportive network.

— *June E. Gabler*

There must be a complete meeting of the minds.
Discord is not permitted.

— *Napoleon Hill*

FEBRUARY 7

A burning purpose attracts others who are
drawn along with it and help fulfill it.
— *Margaret Bourke-White*

A Master Mind Alliance, properly conducted,
stimulates each mind in the alliance to move
with enthusiasm, personal initiative, and
imagination and accelerates the capacity of the
minds in the alliance to receive and transmit
thought vibrations through telepathy and the
sixth sense.
— *Napoleon Hill*

FEBRUARY 8

We should acknowledge differences, we should
greet differences, until difference makes no
difference anymore.
— *Dr. Adela A. Allen*

The Master Mind principle, when actively
applied, has the effect of connecting the
subconscious sections of the minds of the
allies, and gives each member full access to the
spiritual powers of all the other members.
— *Napoleon Hill*

FEBRUARY 9

The greatest gift of human beings is that we
have the power of empathy.

— *Meryl Streep*

It is a matter of established record that all
individual successes, based upon any kind of
achievement above mediocrity, are attained
through the Master Mind principle.

— *Napoleon Hill*

FEBRUARY 10

When we speak of informal leadership, we
describe . . . the capacity of the organization to
create the leadership that best suits its needs at
the time.

— *Meg Wheatley*

One type of Master Mind is for purely social or
personal reasons, consisting of one's relatives,
friends and religious advisers, where no material
gain is sought.

— *Napoleon Hill*

FEBRUARY 11

Never one thing and seldom one person can
make for a success. It takes a number of them
merging into one perfect whole.

— *Marie Dressler*

The other type of Master Mind is the
occupational, business or professional alliance,
consisting of individuals who have a motive of
a material or financial nature; in other words,
an economic alliance, designed to help you sell
your personal services, your skill, your ability, or
to help you succeed in business.

— *Napoleon Hill*

FEBRUARY 12

Our ability to connect our energy, our hearts,
our presence, our intuition, and our healing to
other beings is perhaps our greatest resource.
Once we master the element of contact, we can
heal others as we are being healed.

— *Laura Day*

There are Twelve Great Riches that individuals
aspire to in life. They are: a positive mental
attitude, sound physical health, harmony in
human relationships, freedom from fear, the
hope of achievement, the capacity for faith,
willingness to share one's blessings, a labor
of love, an open mind on all subjects,
self-discipline, the capacity to understand
people, and financial security.

— *Napoleon Hill*

February 13

Speak to yourself as if what you desire is already
true and it already is.

— *Ruth Ross Ressler*

Step 1: Adopt a Definite Purpose as an objective
to be attained by the alliance choosing individual
members whose education, experience, and
influence are such as to make them of the
greatest value in achieving that purpose.

— *Napoleon Hill*

February 14

Don't go to your grave without flying a kite,
skipping rope, going barefoot, catching fireflies,
and jumping in a mud puddle. Let go and live.

— *Barbara Jenkins*

Step 2: Determine what appropriate benefit
each member may receive in return for her
cooperation in the alliance.

— *Napoleon Hill*

FEBRUARY 15

A soul occupied with great ideas best performs
small duties.

— Harriet Martineau

Step 3: Establish a definite place where the
members of the alliance will meet, have a
definite plan, and arrange a definite time for the
mutual discussion of the plan.

— Napoleon Hill

FEBRUARY 16

To do good things in the world, first you must
know who you are and what gives meaning to
your life.

— Paula P. Brownlee

Step 4: It is the burden of the leader of the
alliance to see that harmony among all the
members is maintained and that action is
continuous in the pursuance of the Definite
Major Objective.

— Napoleon Hill

It is difficult to see things clearly if
the shadow of doubt diminishes the
light entering your eyes.

— *Sophia Bedford-Pierce*

Step 5: The watchword of the alliance should be
Definiteness of Purpose, Positiveness of Plan,
backed by continuous perfect harmony.

— *Napoleon Hill*

FEBRUARY 18

Goals are a joint effort process: getting in
touch with our heart and setting a course; then
depending on and being willing for God to
direct us one step at a time.

— *Sheila West*

Step 6: The number of individuals in an alliance
should be governed entirely by the nature and
magnitude of the purpose to be attained.

— *Napoleon Hill*

FEBRUARY 19

After all is said and done, relationships are truly
the only things that really matter.

— Lee Ezell

Begin at once to establish a true Master Mind
Alliance. Select individuals you accept and
who accept you. Do not choose someone just
because you like her.

— Napoleon Hill

FEBRUARY 20

My mission is to travel globally extracting
diamonds out of people's dust.

— Thelma L. Wells

When the members of your alliance
have been selected, take them into your
absolute confidence regarding your
purposes and plans.

— Napoleon Hill

FEBRUARY 21

Leave old or new ideas where they prove
harmful. Leave the bad for the good. Leave
good things for better things.

> — *Barbara Roberts Pine*

Don't tell any one else of the alliance. Reveal
your desires and plans only to the members of
your Master Mind Alliance.

> — *Napoleon Hill*

FEBRUARY 22

Freedom is not the right to do what we want
but the power to do what we ought.

> — *Corrie Ten Boom*

Work out a schedule for contacting
each other frequently.

> — *Napoleon Hill*

FEBRUARY 23

In great moments life seems neither right
nor wrong, but something greater,
it seems inevitable.

— Margaret Sherwood

At each meeting have a report of your individual
and collective progress toward the goal.

— Napoleon Hill

FEBRUARY 24

You don't manage people; you manage things.
You lead people.

— Admiral Grace Hopper

At the first sign of any lack of harmony among
the members, find out what is causing it.

— Napoleon Hill

FEBRUARY 25

Without the burden of afflictions it is impossible
to reach the height of grace. The gifts of grace
increase as the struggles increase.

— *Saint Rose of Lima*

If the negative attitude of any particular member
is causing the lack of harmony, deal with the
problem at once.

— *Napoleon Hill*

FEBRUARY 26

The biggest handicap in the world is
negative thinking.

— *Heather Whitestone*

If required, remove the negative member from
the group. Otherwise, convert the member to
the principles of this philosophy.

— *Napoleon Hill*

FEBRUARY 27

Each person grows not only by her own talents
or development of her inner beliefs, but also by
what she receives from the persons around her.

— *Iris Haberli*

Keep your mind positive and receptive at all
times. Especially when you appear before your
Master Mind group.

— *Napoleon Hill*

FEBRUARY 28

Whenever people think of success, they
immediately think of "more"—more love, more
fun and good times, more respect. Yet, upon
examination, success is not about having more.
It is about fine-tuning your understanding of
what you are willing to give up in order to get
what you really want.

— *Chin-Ning Chu*

Get on good terms with yourself as you work to
develop a successful Master Mind Alliance
with others.

— *Napoleon Hill*

Applied
Faith

Faith is an active state of mind. This belief in yourself is applied to achieving a definite major purpose in life. Faith is an abstract idea, a purely mental concept. Faith is the activity of individual minds facing themselves and establishing a working association with Infinite Intelligence. When a plan comes through to your conscious mind while you are open to the guidance of Infinite Intelligence, accept it with appreciation and gratitude and act on it at once. Do not hesitate, do not argue, challenge, worry, fret about it, or wonder if it's right. Act on it! Action is the first requirement of all faith. As the Bible states: "Faith without works is dead."

Applied Faith generates appropriate resourcefulness from within and augments mastery and competence.

—*Therese G. Sullivan*

MARCH 1

I took an inventory and looked into my little
bag to see what I had left over. I had one
jewel left in the bag, the brightest jewel
of all. I had the gift of faith.

— *Lola Falana*

Faith is a state of mind which you may
develop by conditioning your mind to receive
Infinite Intelligence.

— *Napoleon Hill*

MARCH 2

Nothing contributes so much to tranquilizing
the mind as a steady purpose—a point on which
the soul may fix its intellectual eye.

— *Mary Wollstonecraft Shelley*

Applied faith is adapting the power received
from Infinite Intelligence to a
Definite Major Purpose.

— *Napoleon Hill*

MARCH 3

Throughout the centuries there were men who
took first steps down new roads armed with
nothing but their own vision.

— *Ayn Rand*

Faith is the state of mind in which you contact
the power of Infinite Intelligence and focus it
upon the object of your desire.

— *Napoleon Hill*

MARCH 4

Sorrow looks back. Worry looks round.
Faith looks ahead.

— *Beatrice Fallon*

Faith is a state of mind wherein you temporarily
relax your reason and will power, and open your
mind completely to the guidance of Infinite
Intelligence for the attainment of some
definite purpose.

— *Napoleon Hill*

MARCH 5

Not truth, but faith, it is, that keeps the
world alive.

— *Edna St. Vincent Millay*

The guidance comes in the form of an idea or
plan which comes to you while you are in this
receptive attitude.

— *Napoleon Hill*

MARCH 6

But in this season it is well to reassert that the
hope of mankind rests in faith.
As man thinketh, so he is. Nothing much
happens unless you believe in it, and believing
there is hope for the world is a
way to move toward it.

— *Gladys Taber*

The subconscious mind is the gateway between
our conscious mind and the vast reservoir of
Infinite Intelligence.

— *Napoleon Hill*

MARCH 7

There is nothing to fear except the persistent
refusal to find out the truth, the persistent
refusal to analyze the causes of happenings.
Fear grows in darkness; if you think there's a
bogeyman around, turn on the light.

— *Dorothy Thompson*

The power of Infinite Intelligence pours life
into us as a flowing stream, maintaining all of
the functions of our bodies and minds, and we
can use it to guide and govern the circumstances
and conditions of our lives, if we will act as
conductors of this energy and shape it according
to our constructive purposes.

— *Napoleon Hill*

MARCH 8

To have faith where you cannot see; to be
willing to work on in the dark; to be conscious
of the fact that, so long as you strive for the
best, there are better things on the way, this in
itself is success.

— *Katherine Logan*

If you would have faith—keep your mind on
that which you want and off that
which you do not want.

— *Napoleon Hill*

. . . There are more awakenings than births
in a life.

— *Dorothy Thompson*

Steps to Faith:
* Express a definite desire for the achievement
  of a purpose and relate it to one or more of
  the basic motives.
* Create a definite and specific plan for the
  attainment of that desire.
* Start acting on that plan, putting every
  conscious effort behind it.

— *Napoleon Hill*

MARCH 10

The things that matter the most in this world,
they can never be held in our hand.

— *Gloria Gaither*

When the plan comes through to your
conscious mind, accept it with appreciation and
gratitude and act on it at once!

— *Napoleon Hill*

MARCH 11

Aspire to be, and all that we are not God will
give us credit for trying.

— *Nannie Burroughs*

Accept with gratitude a plan by means of which
you can fulfill your desires through
the rule of hard work backed by a
burning desire.

— *Napoleon Hill*

MARCH 12

Aspiration is the seed of life.

— *Joan Chittister*

You must give an equivalent value for the object
of your desires!

— *Napoleon Hill*

MARCH 13

After all it is those who have a deep and real
inner life who are best able to deal with the
irritating details of outer life.

— *Evelyn Underhill*

When you pray, make your prayer an expression
of gratitude and thanksgiving for the blessings
you have already received.

— *Napoleon Hill*

MARCH 14

The passage is through, not over, not by, not
around, but through.

— *Cherrie Moraga*

To succeed in life you must rid yourself of the
negative influences of fear before faith can
come into your mind.

— *Napoleon Hill*

MARCH 15

Sometimes when you think you are done, it is
just the edge of beginning. Probably that's why
we decide we're done. It's getting scary. We
are touching down onto something real. It is
beyond the point when you think you are done
that often something strong comes out.

— Natalie Goldberg

Fear of poverty is the most destructive of fears
and also the most difficult to master.

— Napoleon Hill

MARCH 16

We know God wipes away all tears,
but it certainly feels good when
He uses human hands.

— Mary Paulson-Lauda

Fear of criticism is almost as general as the fear
of poverty.

— Napoleon Hill

March 17

When you come to the edge of all the light
you know, and are about to step off into the
darkness of the unknown, faith is knowing
one of two things will happen: there will be
something solid to stand on, or you will be
taught how to fly.

— *Barbara J. Winter*

Fear of ill health is related to the fear of death.
There is overwhelming evidence that a disease
can originate as a negative thought which the
person continues to sell to herself until through
autosuggestion physical symptoms
actually appear.

— *Napoleon Hill*

March 18

Put even the plainest woman into a beautiful
dress and unconsciously she will try to live up
to it.

— *Lady Duff-Gordon*

Most doctors now agree that there is a definite
relationship between the patient's mental
attitude and her physical condition.

— *Napoleon Hill*

MARCH 19

I think wholeness comes from living your life
consciously during the day and then exploring
your inner life or unconscious at night.

— *Margery Cuyler*

You can guarantee yourself sound physical
health by maintaining a positive mental attitude
and developing a sound health consciousness
whereby you expect, demand and receive health-
sustaining elements from your food, the fresh
air and sunshine!

— *Napoleon Hill*

MARCH 20

Don't spend time beating on a wall, hoping to
transform it into a door.

— *Dr. Laura Schlessinger*

Fear of the loss of love is the basis of jealousy
and overly-dependent relationships.

— *Napoleon Hill*

MARCH 21

I never feel age . . . . If you have creative work,
you don't have age or time.

— Louise Nevelson

Fear of old age is related to a person's
need to be needed.

— Napoleon Hill

MARCH 22

I make the most of all that comes, and the
least of all that goes.

— Sara Teasdale

Fear of loss of liberty is related to a person's
need to feel independent and autonomous.

— Napoleon Hill

MARCH 23

Begin doing what you want to do now. We are not living in eternity. We have only this moment, sparkling like a star in our hand—and melting like a snowflake. Let us use it before it is too late.

— *Marie Beyon Ray*

Fear of death is a universal fear and seems related to a person's need to feel a sense of worth validated by continued life.

— *Napoleon Hill*

MARCH 24

You can have anything you want if you want it desperately enough. You must want it with an inner exuberance that erupts through the skin and joins the energy that created the world.

— *Sheila Graham*

The mind attracts to it the counterpart of that which it dwells upon.

— *Napoleon Hill*

MARCH 25

I invented my life by taking for granted that
everything I did not like would have an opposite
which I would like.

— *Coco Chanel*

Before the state of mind known as faith will
produce practical results, it must be expressed in
some form of action.

— *Napoleon Hill*

MARCH 26

For you to be successful, sacrifices must be
made. It's better that they are made by others
but failing that, you'll have to make
them yourself.

— *Rita Mae Brown*

Faith is the act of believing by doing.

— *Napoleon Hill*

MARCH 27

People always call it luck when you've acted
more sensibly than they have.

— *Anne Tyler*

One of the greatest things you can do with
applied faith is to refuse to think about things
you do not want and feed your mind on the
things you do want until you start getting them.

— *Napoleon Hill*

MARCH 28

At the worst, a house unkept cannot be so
distressing as a life unlived.

— *Dame Rose Macaulay*

Faith without works is dead.

— *Napoleon Hill*

MARCH 29

Life is about not knowing, having to change,
taking the moment and making the best of it,
without knowing what's going to happen next.
Delicious ambiguity.

— Gilda Radner

Faith can give you the strength to move through
temporary defeat.

— Napoleon Hill

MARCH 30

With faith as my crutch I've found peace,
one of the few things I have left which is
strictly my own.

— Nancy Reagan

Faith can tune you into the possibilities existing
even within defeat.

— Napoleon Hill

MARCH 31

When you can't have what you want, it's time to
start wanting what you have.

— *Kathleen A. Sutton*

Faith can help you discover that every adversity
carries with it the seed of an equivalent or
greater benefit.

— *Napoleon Hill*

Going the
Extra Mile

Going the Extra Mile is the action of rendering more and better service than that for which you are presently paid. When you Go The Extra Mile, the Law of Compensation comes into play. This Universal Law neither permits any living thing to get something for nothing nor allows any form of labor to go unrewarded. You will find that Mother Nature goes the extra mile in everything that she does. She doesn't create just barely enough of each gene or species to get by; she produces an over abundance to take care of all emergencies that arise and still have enough left to guarantee the perpetuation of each form of life.

. . . taking the initiative came naturally to me. It wasn't until my adult years that I realized how far my initiative had taken me in life.

— Maureen E. Muha

APRIL 1

Let no one come to you without leaving better.

— *Mother Teresa*

Going the Extra Mile places the Law of
Increasing Returns at your command and
working for your benefit.

— *Napoleon Hill*

APRIL 2

If we keep on doin' what we always done, we'll
keep on gettin' what we always got.

— *Barbara Lyon*

The habit of doing more than that for which
you are being paid causes you to benefit by the
Law of Compensation through which no act
or deed will or can be expressed without an
equivalent reaction after its own kind.

— *Napoleon Hill*

APRIL 3

If someone listens, or stretches out a hand,
or whispers a kind word of encouragement,
or attempts to understand a lonely person,
extraordinary things begin to happen.

— Loretta Girzartis

You must render the greatest amount of service
of which you are capable and render it in a
friendly, positive manner.

— Napoleon Hill

APRIL 4

Do not save your loving speeches
For your friends till they are dead;
Do not write them on their tombstones,
Speak them rather now instead.

— Anna Cummins

You must do this regardless of your immediate
compensation—even if it appears that you will
receive no immediate compensation whatsoever!

— Napoleon Hill

April 5

An effort made for the happiness of others
lifts us above ourselves.

— *Lydia M. Child*

Until a man begins to render more service than
that for which he is paid, he is not entitled to
more pay than he receives for that service, since,
obviously, he is already receiving full pay for
what he does!

— *Napoleon Hill*

April 6

Great opportunities to help others seldom
come, but small ones surround us every day.

— *Sally Koch*

98 out of 100 wage earners have no Definite
Purpose greater than that of working for a daily
wage. Therefore, no matter how much work
they do, or how well they do it, the "wheel of
fortune" turns past them without giving them
more than a bare living, because they neither
expect nor demand more!

— *Napoleon Hill*

APRIL 7

Little deeds of kindness, little words of love,
Help to make earth happy like the heaven above.
                              — *Julia A. Fletcher Carney*

The habit of doing more than you are paid for
will bring you to the favorable attention of those
who have opportunities to offer.
                              — *Napoleon Hill*

APRIL 8

For life is the mirror of king and slave,
'Tis just what we are and do;
Then give to the world the best you have,
And the best will come back to you.
                              — *Madeleine Bridges*

You will never command more than average
compensation until you become indispensable
to somebody or some group.
                              — *Napoleon Hill*

APRIL 9

No man is better than his service for the
betterment of others.

— *Candice M. Pope*

Going the Extra Mile leads to your mental
growth and physical perfection in various forms
of service, thereby developing a greater ability
and skill in your chosen vocation.

— *Napoleon Hill*

APRIL 10

You have to recognize when the right place and
the right time fuse and take advantage of that
opportunity. There are plenty of opportunities
out there. You can't sit back and wait.

— *Ellen Metcalf*

Going the Extra Mile protects you against the
loss of employment and places you in a position
to choose your own job and working conditions.

— *Napoleon Hill*

APRIL 11

If you really want something, you can
figure out how to make it happen.

— Cher

Going the Extra Mile turns the spotlight on
you and gives you the benefit of the Law of
Contrast, which is very important
in advertising yourself.

— Napoleon Hill

APRIL 12

Life is not easy for any of us. But what of that?
We must have perseverance and above all
confidence in ourselves. We must believe that
we are gifted for something and that this thing,
at whatever cost, must be attained.

— Madame Curie

Doing more than you are immediately paid for
leads to the development of a positive, pleasing
attitude, which is among the more important
traits of a Pleasing Personality.

— Napoleon Hill

April 13

When we deliberately leave the safety of the
shore of our lives, we surrender to a
mystery beyond our intent.

— *Ann Linnea*

Going the Extra Mile definitely gives you greater
confidence in yourself and puts you on a better
basis with your own conscience.

— *Napoleon Hill*

April 14

You can't build a reputation on what you
intend to do.

— *Liz Smith*

Going the Extra Mile aids one in overcoming
the destructive habit of procrastination.

— *Napoleon Hill*

April 15

Great thoughts speak only to the thoughtful
mind, but great actions speak to all mankind.

— *Emily P. Bissell*

Going the Extra Mile helps you develop
Definiteness of Purpose, without which one
cannot hope for success.

— *Napoleon Hill*

April 16

This has always been a motto of mine:
Attempt the impossible in order
to improve your work.

— *Bette Davis*

If you never do anything more than you get
paid for, you'll never get paid for anything
more than you do.

— *Napoleon Hill*

APRIL 17

Life is change. Growth is optional.
Choose wisely.

— *Karen Kaiser Clark*

The habit of Going the Extra Mile is one
which you may adopt and follow on your own
initiative without asking the permission of
anyone to do so.

— *Napoleon Hill*

APRIL 18

Women share with men the need for personal
success, even the taste for power, and no longer
are we willing to satisfy those needs through the
achievements of surrogates, whether husbands,
children, or merely role models.

— *Elizabeth Dole*

Quality of service rendered + Quantity of
service rendered + the Mental Attitude in which
it is rendered = your compensation.

— *Napoleon Hill*

APRIL 19

When we are magnanimous, liberal in
our giving as well as in sharing of our self,
we show noble character and an abundance
of spirit and strength.

— Alexandra Stoddard

$Q^1 + Q^2 + MA = $ Compensation

— Napoleon Hill

APRIL 20

I refuse to believe that trading recipes is silly.
Tunafish casserole is at least as real as
corporate stock.

— Barbara Grizzuti Harrison

Each time you perform an act with the attitude
that you are going to excel all of your previous
achievements you are really growing.

— Napoleon Hill

APRIL 21

Striving for excellence motivates you;
striving for perfection is demoralizing.

— *Harriet Braiker*

Going the Extra Mile is one way of writing
yourself an insurance policy against the fear of
poverty, fear of want, and against the low pay
competition of the "clock watcher."

— *Napoleon Hill*

APRIL 22

One must think like a hero to behave like a
merely decent human being.

— *May Sarton*

Going the Extra Mile turns the spotlight on
you and gives you the benefit of the Law of
Contrast, a good way to advertise yourself.

— *Napoleon Hill*

April 23

From where you sit, you can probably reach
out with comparative ease and touch a life of
serenity and peace. You can wait for things to
happen and not get too sad when they don't.
That's fine for some but not for me. Serenity is
pleasant, but it lacks the ecstasy of achievement.

— *Estee Lauder*

The habit of rendering more and better service
than you are immediately compensated for
develops the habit of Personal Initiative.

— *Napoleon Hill*

April 24

Happiness is not a station to arrive at. But a
manner of traveling.

— *Margaret Lee Runbeck*

Personal Initiative means doing the thing
that needs to be done without somebody
telling you to do it.

— *Napoleon Hill*

April 25

The only place you'll find success before
work is in the dictionary.

— *May B. Smith*

Don't wait for things to happen, make
them happen.

— *Napoleon Hill*

April 26

The way I see it, if you want the rainbow, you've
got to be willing to put up with the rain.

— *Dolly Parton*

You know, sometimes the hardest gal in the
world to get along with is the one walking
around under your own hat.

— *Napoleon Hill*

APRIL 27

The great thing to learn about life is, first, not to
do what you don't want to do, and, second, to
do what you do want to do.

— *Margaret Anderson*

It pays to be on good terms with your
own conscious.

— *Napoleon Hill*

APRIL 28

The more we give of anything, the more we
shall get back.

— *Grace Speare*

You must do what you are paid for, to keep the
job, but you have the privilege of rendering an
overplus of service as a means of accumulating a
reserve credit of goodwill which entitles you to
higher pay and a better position.

— *Napoleon Hill*

APRIL 29

As long as you keep a person down, some part
of you has to be down there to hold him down,
so it means you cannot soar as you
otherwise might.

— Marian Anderson

If the type of service you are trained to render
does not bring the compensation
you feel that you require, then possibly you
should consider a change of occupation.

— Napoleon Hill

APRIL 30

When it comes to getting things done, we need
fewer architects and more bricklayers.

— Colleen C. Barrett

The habit of Going the Extra Mile is one
which you may adopt and follow on your own
initiative, without asking the permission of
anyone to do so.

— Napoleon Hill

Pleasing
Personality

Personality is the sum total of one's mental, spiritual, and physical traits and habits that distinguish one from all others. It is the factor that determines whether one is liked or disliked by others. Your personality is your greatest asset or liability. It embraces everything you control—mind, body and soul. Some characteristics of a pleasing personality include: positive mental attitude, flexibility, sincerity, prompt actions, courtesy, tactfulness, pleasing tone of voice, smile, and tolerance.

In my experience having a pleasing personality is really about being conscious of those around you, really caring about what is important to them.

— *Adora Spencer*

MAY 1

There's always room for improvement—
it's the biggest room in the house.

— *Louise Heath Leber*

Every person achieving a high degree of
personal success has mastered the art of
successfully selling herself.

— *Napoleon Hill*

MAY 2

Having harvested all the knowledge and wisdom
we can from our mistakes and failures, we
should put them behind us and go ahead, for
vain regretting interferes with the flow of power
into our own personalities.

— *Edith Johnson*

Persons possessing a pleasing personality
attract success. They turn on others.
Sour souls, know-it-alls, and negative persons
only attract failure and they are real turn-offs.

— *Napoleon Hill*

MAY 3

Make it happen; don't watch it happen.
— *Diane R. Vaughn*

A Positive Mental Attitude heads the list as the
most important trait necessary in developing
a Pleasing Personality. Positive is more than
merely the opposite of negative. It means having
assurance, confidence, a belief in self, a feeling
of rightness, and a belief in one's capacity to
achieve one's Definite Major Purpose.
— *Napoleon Hill*

MAY 4

There are two ways of spreading light: to be the
candle or the mirror that reflects it.
— *Edith Wharton*

Flexibility consists in the habit of adapting one's
self to quickly changing circumstances without
losing one's sense of composure or confidence.
— *Napoleon Hill*

May 5

Kindness is always fashionable.

— Amelia E. Barr

Courtesy is the habit of rendering useful service
without the expectation of direct reward, the
habit of respecting other people's feelings under
all circumstances, the habit of going out of one's
way if need be to help any less fortunate person
whenever possible, and last, but not least, the
habit of controlling selfishness, and greed, and
envy, and hatred.

— Napoleon Hill

May 6

As novices, we think we're entirely responsible
for the way people treat us. I have long since
learned that we are responsible only for the way
we treat people.

— Rose Lane

People who like people are usually liked by
others. People who dislike others generally are
not liked by others.

— Napoleon Hill

MAY 7

Of all the things you wear, your expression
is the most important.

— *Janet Lane*

The Habit of Smiling is directly related to a
Positive Mental Attitude. It's a reflection of faith
and joy. If you do not possess this trait, you
should begin immediately practicing before a
mirror. Smiling and success go together hand
in hand.

— *Napoleon Hill*

MAY 8

The best index to a person's character is
(a) how he treats people who can't do him any
good, and (b) how he treats people who can't
fight back.

— *Abigail Van Buren*

Tolerance consists of an open mind on all
subjects, toward all people, at all times.
In addition to being one of the more important
of the traits of a pleasing personality, an open
mind on all subjects is one of the Twelve Great
Riches of Life.

— *Napoleon Hill*

MAY 9

You never saw a fish on the wall with its
mouth shut.

— *Sally Berger*

Tactfulness consists in doing and saying the
right thing at the right time.

— *Napoleon Hill*

MAY 10

We are rich only through what we give;
and poor only through what we refuse
and keep.

— *Anne Swetchine*

Sincerity begins with you. The woman who is
sincere with others must first be sincere
with herself.

— *Napoleon Hill*

May 11

Civility costs nothing and buys everything.
— *Mary Whortley Montague*

While we have no tails to wag, our face, with its
many muscles and numerous possible shapes,
serves as a mirror of one's self, reflecting the
inner woman. As such, the smile, the tone of
voice, and the expression of the face constitute
open windows through which others may see
our inner selves.

— *Napoleon Hill*

May 12

It is easy to be popular. It is not easy to be just.
— *Rose Elizabeth Bird*

Women of sound character always have the
courage to deal directly and openly with others
and they follow this habit even though it may
at times be to their disadvantage. However,
honesty yields fewer regrets than dishonesty,
and it creates a soundness of mind and
spirit which comes through the practice of
maintaining a clear conscience.

— *Napoleon Hill*

May 13

I didn't belong as a kid, and that always
bothered me. If only I'd known that one day my
differentness would be an asset, then my early
life would have been much easier.

— *Bette Midler*

Humility of the heart is a sign of great inner
strength and confidence.

— *Napoleon Hill*

May 14

When death, the great reconciler, has come,
it is never our tenderness that we repent of,
but our severity.

— *George Eliot*

Watch your tongue. It has no mind of its own.
Keep it within your cheek and keep your brain
in charge of your mouth.

— *Napoleon Hill*

MAY 15

On the banks of the James River, a husband
erected a tombstone in memory of his wife,
one of those 100 maidens who had come to
Virginia in 1619 to marry the lonely settlers. The
stone bore this legend: "She touched the soil of
Virginia with her little foot and the wilderness
became a home."

— Eudora R. Richardson

Life, from birth until death, is dependent to a
large degree upon salesmanship.

— Napoleon Hill

MAY 16

Every small, positive change we can make
in ourselves repays us in confidence in
the future.

— Alice Walker

Humor is a sign of faith and is the product of
a Positive Mental Attitude. Humor guards one
against being overcome by fear and failure. It
gives a bounce to life and the human spirit.

— Napoleon Hill

Personal
Initiative

"There are two types of men," said Andrew Carnegie, "who never amount to anything. One is the fellow who never does anything except that which he is told to do, the other is the fellow who never does more than he is told to do. The man who gets ahead does the thing that should be done without being told to do it, but he does not stop there, he goes the extra mile by doing a great deal more than is expected or demanded of him." Personal Initiative is the power that inspires the completion of that which one begins. It is the power that starts all action. No person is free until he learns to do his own thinking and gains the courage to act on his own Personal Initiative—it is the twin brother of Going the Extra Mile.

Our ability to do this—to perform a role we are no longer enthusiastically committed to—is one of our acquired talents.

— *Diane R. Vaughn*

May 17

Learning is not attained by chance; it must
be sought for with ardor and attended to
with diligence.

— Abigail Adams

Personal Initiative bears the same relationship
to an individual that a self-starter bears to an
automobile. It is the power that inspires the
completion of that which one begins. There are
many starters among women, but there are
few finishers.

— Napoleon Hill

May 18

The percentage of mistakes in quick decisions is
no greater than in long-drawn out vacillations,
and the effect of decisiveness itself "makes
things go" and creates confidence.

— Anne O'Hare McCormick

Personal Initiative reveals favorable
opportunities for self-advancement and inspires
one to embrace them and realize
their full potential.

— Napoleon Hill

MAY 19

To get anywhere, strike out for somewhere,
or you'll get nowhere.

— *Martha Lupton*

Women with Personal Initiative do not drift
aimlessly, but sail boldly out across the seas of
personal success.

— *Napoleon Hill*

MAY 20

It is better to protest than to accept injustice.

— *Rosa Parks*

Therefore, if you would be done with the
negative side of the street then prepare yourself
to cross over and begin walking down the
avenue named Positive. Move on your
Personal Initiative.

— *Napoleon Hill*

One sure window into a person's soul is
his reading list.

— *Mary B. W. Tabor*

The mind that has been made ready to
receive attracts that which it needs, just as an
electromagnet attracts steel filings.

— *Napoleon Hill*

MAY 22

The key to whatever success I enjoy today
is: Don't ask. Do.

— *Vikki Carr*

The most difficult part of any task is that of
making a start at performing it.

— *Napoleon Hill*

MAY 23

If you don't want to get tackled, don't
carry the ball.

— *Ann McKay Thompson*

Winners are those persons who get in the game
and dare to compete for the prize of
life's great riches.

— *Napoleon Hill*

❦

MAY 24

You may be disappointed if you fail, but you are
doomed if you don't try.

— *Beverly Sills*

There is always the tendency to wait for a better
day or for that moment described as when the
"time is right." However, once a start has been
made, the power of performance presents itself.

— *Napoleon Hill*

MAY 25

Never fear shadows. They simply mean that
there's a light somewhere nearby.

— *Ruth E. Renkei*

Adopt a Definite Major Purpose and see how
quickly the habit of moving on your own
Personal Initiative will inspire you to action in
carrying out the object of your purpose.

— *Napoleon Hill*

MAY 26

Too often, the opportunity knocks, but by the
time you push back the chain, push back the
bolt, unhook the two locks and shut off the
burglar alarm, it's too late.

— *Rita Coolidge*

In conclusion, it should be pointed out once
more that few games are ever won by players
sitting on the sidelines. If you want to win at life
you then must get involved.

— *Napoleon Hill*

MAY 27

Opportunities are usually disguised as hard
work, so most people don't recognize them.

— Ann Landers

You must be willing to pay the price of success,
and that usually can be translated into such
terms as: sweat and strain, tears and toil, hope
and hurt, brains and brawn.

— Napoleon Hill

MAY 28

My mother drew a distinction between
achievement and success. She said,
"Achievement is the knowledge that you have
studied and worked hard and done the best that
is in you. Success is being praised by others,
and that's nice, too, but not as important or
satisfying." Always aim for achievement and
forget about success.

— Helen Hayes

Success is reserved for those persons who are
dedicated to the proposition that achievers are
doers and that success comes to those who are
about the business of succeeding in life.

— Napoleon Hill

MAY 29

I decided to be a human being and not a role.

— *Sonia Johnson*

Somewhere along the way you will meet your
"other self" face to face—that which can and
will carry you over onto the successful side of
the street.

— *Napoleon Hill*

MAY 30

To realize originality one has to have the
courage to be an amateur.

— *Marianne Moore*

Never mind how much you know.
The important thing is what you can
do with what you know!

— *Napoleon Hill*

MAY 31

Growth demands a temporary surrender
of security.

> — *Gail Sheehy*

Winners are self-starters. They are action-
oriented, always taking the initiative. They do
not wait on success, but are continually moving
in the direction of realizing life goals.

> — *Napoleon Hill*

Positive Mental Attitude

Positive Mental Attitude is the right mental attitude in all circumstances. Keep your mind on the things you want and off the things you don't want. Remember the old French proverb: "Be very careful what you set your heart on, for you will surely achieve it." Success attracts more success while failure attracts more failure. This principle presents the means by which the entire philosophy can best be assimilated and put to practical use. You cannot get the most out of the other sixteen principles without understanding and applying this one.

With a Positive Mental Attitude, knowing my shortcomings doesn't bring me down, rather, it helps me to decide what to do about it.

— *Marie Hejnal*

JUNE 1

The greater part of our happiness or misery
depends upon our dispositions, and not
our circumstances.

— *Martha Washington*

Thoughts are powerful.

— *Napoleon Hill*

JUNE 2

I'm not going to die, I'm going home
like a shooting star.

— *Sojourner Truth*

Ideas can capture the human spirit, move the
masses, and turn an entire society about face.

— *Napoleon Hill*

June 3

Cheerfulness, if would appear, is a matter which
depends fully as much on the state of things
within, as on the state of things without and
around us.

—Charlotte Brontë

Remember: "As a man thinketh in his
heart, so is he."

— Napoleon Hill

June 4

Why compare yourself to others? No one in the
entire world can do a better job than you.

— Susan Carlson

Any woman who takes herself seriously and
dares to think the thoughts of personal growth
and gain must add the creative catalyst of a
Positive Mental Attitude.

— Napoleon Hill

JUNE 5

I discovered I always have choices and
sometimes it's only a choice of attitude.

— *Judith M. Knowlton*

An attitude can be described as a
psychological posture.

— *Napoleon Hill*

JUNE 6

One only gets to the top rung on the ladder by
steadily climbing up one at a time, and suddenly,
all sorts of powers, all sorts of abilities which
you thought never belonged to you—suddenly
become within your own possibility and you
think, "Well, I'll have a go, too."

— *Margaret Thatcher*

Self-actualization is an important concept.
Actualization means the transformation of
possibilities into realities. Self-actualization
means reaching deep within yourself and
bringing forth your very best efforts.

— *Napoleon Hill*

JUNE 7

An optimist is the human personification
of spring.

> — *Susan J. Bissonette*

Behind the concept and reality of self-
actualization is a belief in the goodness of
"rightness" of life. This is a positive statement
and affirms that everyone has a place in life and
a right to live life at the fullest.

> — *Napoleon Hill*

JUNE 8

Life is what we make it. Always has been.
Always will be.

> — *Anna Mary (Grandma) Moses*

Remember: Thoughts shape our lives!

> — *Napoleon Hill*

JUNE 9

Life is like a butterfly. You can chase it,
or you can let it come to you.

— *Ruth Brown*

You can take possession of your thought power
or you can let it be influenced by all
the stray winds of chance and undesirable
circumstances.

— *Napoleon Hill*

JUNE 10

Today, see if you can stretch your heart and
expand your love so that it touches not only
those to whom you can give it easily,
but also those who need it so much.

— *Daphne Rose Kingma*

Even in the midst of great adversity, the positive
person tells herself over and over again that life
is good and she can weather the storm.

— *Napoleon Hill*

JUNE 11

Kind words are jewels that live in the heart and
soul and remain as blessed memories years after
they have been spoken.

— Marvea Johnson

The mental in Positive Mental Attitude is
the dynamic of thought which provides for
the continual reinforcement of the feeling of
confidence and belief in one's self.

— Napoleon Hill

JUNE 12

You really have to look inside yourself and
find your own inner strength, and say,
"I'm proud of what I am and who I am,
and I'm just going to be myself."

— Mariah Carey

The woman who has a Positive Mental Attitude
is one who has assumed a life posture which
permits her to confidently face life situations.

— Napoleon Hill

JUNE 13

Optimism is what you do, how you live.

— *Andrea Dworkin*

Our beliefs must be continually reinforced.
The muscles of self-confidence must be
strengthened through a daily workout, mental in
design, so that in the midst of adversity
one will be strong enough to win
in spite of the odds.

— *Napoleon Hill*

JUNE 14

The accumulation of small, optimistic acts
produces quality in our culture and in
your life. Our culture resonates in tense times
to individual acts of grace.

— *Jennifer James*

Peace of mind can only be obtained through a
Positive Mental Attitude. Peace of mind requires
helping others to help themselves.

— *Napoleon Hill*

JUNE 15

Character contributes to beauty. It fortifies a
woman as her youth fades. A mode of conduct,
a standard of courage, discipline, fortitude,
and integrity can do a great deal to make a
woman beautiful.

— *Jacqueline Bisset*

A Positive Mental Attitude is the first and the
most important step we must take in the control
and direction of our minds since all degrees of
a negative mental attitude leave us wide open to
every negative influence we contact.

— *Napoleon Hill*

JUNE 16

Perseverance is failing nineteen times and
succeeding the twentieth.

— *Julie Andrews*

You can develop a Positive Mental
Attitude by selecting a pace-maker, and
emulating her.

— *Napoleon Hill*

JUNE 17

Courage is the atom of change.

— *Jacqueline Bisset*

It is important to realize that the great crime of
the universe is stagnation.

— *Napoleon Hill*

JUNE 18

Nobody really cares if you are miserable,
so you might as well be happy.

— *Cythina Nelms*

Positive Mental Attitude is the only condition of
the mind in which we can express Applied Faith
and draw upon the forces of Infinite Intelligence.

— *Napoleon Hill*

JUNE 19

A strong, positive self-image is the best possible
preparation for success.

— *Dr. Joyce Brothers*

Positive Mental Attitude is the only
condition which permits us to get on the
Success Beam.

— *Napoleon Hill*

JUNE 20

Invest in the human soul. Who knows, it might
be a diamond in the rough.

— *Mary McLeod Bethune*

Positive Mental Attitude is the only condition of
the mind in which we can meet and recognize our
"other self"—that self which has no limitations.

— *Napoleon Hill*

June 21

Be on the alert to recognize your prime at
whatever time of life it may occur.

— *Muriel Spark*

Remember that no one is ever rewarded or
promoted because of a bad disposition and a
negative mental attitude.

— *Napoleon Hill*

June 22

Look at everything as though you were seeing it
either for the first or last time. Then your time
on earth will be filled with glory.

— *Betty Smith*

To maintain the feeling of confidence, there
must be repetitious thought charged with
assurance and belief itself.

— *Napoleon Hill*

JUNE 23

I'm looking forward to looking back on all this.
— Sandra Knell

Individuals with positive mental attitudes
are never found in a rut.
— Napoleon Hill

JUNE 24

Beauty is in the eye of the beholder.
— Margaret Wolfe Hungerford

It is the believing woman who achieves.
— Napoleon Hill

JUNE 25

Stinky attitudes are airborne. They waft around and add to the pollution on planet earth. But we don't have to take a deep breath to detect attitudes; they're as obvious as a new pair of iridescent sneakers. Just as surely as we wear our Liz Claibornes and Ralph Laurens, we can be seen strutting, sneaking, and slumping around in our negative 'tudes.

— *Patsy Clairmont*

You can form the habit of tolerance and keep an open mind on all subjects, toward people of all races and creeds, and learn to like people as they are instead of demanding them to be like you.

— *Napoleon Hill*

JUNE 26

There are so many things that we wish we had done yesterday, so few that we feel like doing today.

— *Mignon McLaughlin*

Winners are those persons in life who have taken possession of their minds, exercise control over their thoughts and maintain a Positive Mental Attitude in their quest for success.

— *Napoleon Hill*

JUNE 27

A strong positive attitude will create more
miracles than any wonder drug.

— *Patricia Neal*

You can take possession of your thought power
or you can let it be influenced by all the stray
winds of chance and undesirable circumstances.

— *Napoleon Hill*

❧

JUNE 28

My motto is that I enjoy life. I think there's a
kind of simplicity to that way of thinking.

— *Jenna Elfman*

A Positive Mental Attitude is generated when
a person assumes a confident life-stance which
originates and is sustained through the control
of one's thoughts.

— *Napoleon Hill*

JUNE 29

The only difference between a rut and a
grave is their dimensions.

— *Ellen Glasgow*

Keep your mind on the things you want and off
the things you don't want. Remember the old
French proverb: "Be very careful what you set
your heart on, for you will surely achieve it."

— *Napoleon Hill*

JUNE 30

Humility is not my forte, and whenever I dwell
for any length of time on my own shortcomings,
they gradually begin to seem mild, harmless,
rather engaging little things, not at all like the
staring defects in other people's characters.

— *Margaret Halsey*

Adjust yourself to other people's states of
mind and their peculiarities so as to get along
peacefully with them, and refrain from taking
notice of trivial circumstances in your human
relations by refusing to allow them to become
controversial incidents.

— *Napoleon Hill*

Enthusiasm

Enthusiasm is faith in action. Enthusiasm comes from the Greek words "en" which means "in" and "theos" which means "God." It is the intense emotion known as burning desire. Enthusiasm comes from within, although it radiates outwardly in the expression of one's voice and countenance. Enthusiasm is power because it is the instrument by which adversities and failures and temporary defeats may be transmuted into action backed by faith. The flame of enthusiasm burning within you turns thought into action.

No longer do I have to accept or compromise with less than my own personal expectations.

— *Deanna Davis*

JULY 1

The essence of pleasure is spontaneity.

— *Germaine Greer*

Enthusiasm causes one to glow with
self-confidence.

— *Napoleon Hill*

༄

JULY 2

Life itself is the proper binge.

— *Julia Child*

Enthusiasm definitely takes the drudgery
out of labor.

— *Napoleon Hill*

JULY 3

The sense of the word among the Greeks
affords the noblest definition of it; enthusiasm
signifies "God in us."

— Madame de Stael

Enthusiasm is the utilization of the God
within you and the ability to tap and direct this
tremendous force.

— Napoleon Hill

JULY 4

It's easier to act your way into new ways of
feeling than to feel yourself into new ways
of acting.

— Susan Glaser

Remember, you are developing the habit of
Controlled Enthusiasm and the creation of
habits requires repetition through
physical action.

— Napoleon Hill

July 5

You will do foolish things, but do them
with enthusiasm.

— Colette

Enthusiasm steps up thought vibrations and
stimulates the imagination.

— Napoleon Hill

July 6

It isn't the great pleasures that count the most;
it's making a great deal out of the little ones.

— Jean Webster

Enthusiasm gives a thrust to life,
an impetus toward success.

— Napoleon Hill

JULY 7

Each dawn holds a new hope for a new
plan, making the start of each day the
start of a new life.

— *Gina Blair*

Enthusiasm concentrates the powers of the
mind and gives them the wings of action.

— *Napoleon Hill*

JULY 8

Deep listening from the heart is one half of true
communication. Speaking from the heart is the
other half.

— *Sandra Paddison*

Enthusiasm gives brilliance and color to the
spoken word.

— *Napoleon Hill*

JULY 9

My heart is singing for joy this morning.
A miracle has happened! The light of
understanding has shone upon my little pupil's
mind, and behold, all things are changed!

— *Annie Sullivan*

Enthusiasm is power, because it is the
instrument by which adversities and failures and
temporary defeat may be transmuted into action
backed by faith.

— *Napoleon Hill*

JULY 10

The real power behind whatever success I have
now was something I found within myself—
something that's in all of us,
I think, a little piece of God just waiting
to be discovered.

— *Tina Turner*

Enthusiasm is "faith in action," pushing aside
those obstacles which stand between a woman
and her Definite Major Purpose.

— *Napoleon Hill*

JULY 11

We've stopped counting fireflies at dusk, standing
naked in the rain, finger painting with our feet
and stuffing a bag full of costumes and making
our "poet's corner" in the backyard, with lanterns
and tents made out of chenille bedspreads. We
deserve to be the caretakers for our spirits and
dreams, and this means truly sensing and listening
for our most alive route.

— Sark

Enthusiasm moves mountains, blows apart
negative thoughts, repels the negativism of
others, secures support for your ideas, enlists the
cooperation of others, encourages confidence, and
underscores your sincerity of purpose.

— Napoleon Hill

JULY 12

Light tomorrow with today.

— Elizabeth Barrett Browning

Give a woman a burning desire to achieve a
definite end, and a definite motive setting fire
to that desire and very quickly the flames of
enthusiasm will begin burning and a power will
be generated which, when properly directed,
will assist a person in realizing their
Definite Major Purpose.

— Napoleon Hill

July 13

The bravest thing you can do when you
are not brave is to profess courage and
act accordingly.

— *Corra Harris*

Enthusiasm clears the mind of negative
cobwebs and prepares the way for the "faith in
action" so vital to personal success.

— *Napoleon Hill*

July 14

To look backward for a while is to refresh the
eye, to restore it, and to render it more fit for its
prime function of looking forward.

— *Margaret Fairless Barber*

Remember, enthusiasm thrives on a
positive spirit.

— *Napoleon Hill*

JULY 15

If you want to touch the other shore badly
enough, barring an impossible situation, you
will. If your desire is diluted for any
reason, you'll never make it.

— *Dina Nyad*

Enthusiasm is the "action factor of thought!"
Where it is strong enough, it literally forces
one into action appropriate to the nature of the
motive which inspired it.

— *Napoleon Hill*

Teamwork

Teamwork is harmonious cooperation that is willing, voluntary and free. Whenever the spirit of Teamwork is the dominating influence in business or industry, success is inevitable. Harmonious cooperation is a priceless asset that you can acquire in proportion to your giving. Teamwork, in a spirit of friendliness, costs little in the way of time and effort. Generosity, fair treatment, courtesy, and a willingness to serve are qualities that pay high dividends whenever they are applied in human relations.

If I failed to successfully accomplish my responsibilities, I prevented those who followed me from accomplishing their duties.

— *Dr. Judith B. Arcy*

JULY 16

Imparting knowledge is only lighting other men's candles at our lamp, without depriving ourselves of any flame.

— *Jane Porter*

Cooperation, like love and friendship, is something one receives by giving.

— *Napoleon Hill*

JULY 17

A clay pot sitting in the sun will always be a clay pot. It has to go through the white heat of the furnace to become porcelain.

— *Mildred Stouven*

Underdogs can become winners when they believe themselves capable of winning and are willing to commit themselves to victory.

— *Napoleon Hill*

JULY 18

When people universally realize that all are
united by the common bond of mortality and by
the basic needs . . . the need to worship
and to love, to be housed and fed, to work
and play, perhaps we will have learned to
understand, which is to love spiritually, and
there will be peace and brotherhood on earth.
Without brotherhood, peace is not possible.

— *Faith Baldwin*

Not only does your present and future depend
upon your ability to join hands with others—
but the tomorrow our children will know will
depend upon how willing we are to walk the
road of life together in peace and prosperity as
we build a better world.

— *Napoleon Hill*

JULY 19

Our happiness is greatest when we contribute to
the happiness of others.

— *Harriet Shepard*

The cooperative spirit is a gift which can be
offered to another human being.

— *Napoleon Hill*

JULY 20

Remember, we all stumble, every one of us.
That's why it's a comfort to go hand in hand.

— Emily Kimbrough

The cooperative spirit is also a torch which
can be passed on to another generation,
holding high the light of hope and love,
peace and prosperity.

— Napoleon Hill

JULY 21

Surround yourself only with people who are
going to lift you higher.

— Oprah Winfrey

A cooperative spirit increases your success
potential while benefiting others.

— Napoleon Hill

JULY 22

If I had to characterize one quality as the genius
of feminist thought, culture, and action, it would
be the connectivity.

— *Robin Morgan*

We are not only surrounded by the water of
humanity, but we are connected and joined
together by common concerns, interests and
needs which bind us and create the very ground
of our being and the human experience.

— *Napoleon Hill*

JULY 23

Reinforce the stitch that ties us, and I will
do the same for you.

— *Doris Schwerin*

A contagious enthusiasm is required if a group is
to become "fired-up" and prepared for victory.

— *Napoleon Hill*

July 24

Treat your friends as you do your best pictures,
and place them in their best light.

— *Jennie Jerome Churchill*

Winners win because they believe
winning possible.

— *Napoleon Hill*

July 25

Never refuse any advance of friendship, for if
nine out of ten bring you nothing, one alone
may repay you.

— *Madame de Tencin*

Willing teamwork is the only type that leads to
constructive ends, the only type that sustains the
power of people through coordinated efforts.

— *Napoleon Hill*

JULY 26

Continuous effort—not strength or
intelligence—is the key to unlocking
our potential.

— Liane Cardes

Teamwork produces power, but the question
as to whether the power is temporary or
permanent depends upon the motive that
inspires the cooperation.

— Napoleon Hill

JULY 27

What we plan we build.

— Phoebe Cary

Victory, if it is to be realized, requires
team effort—teamwork.

— Napoleon Hill

July 28

Of any stopping place in life, it is good to ask
whether it will be a good place from which to
go on as well as a good place to remain.

— *Mary Catherine Bateson*

The individual attempting to win at life or the
organization attempting to realize
great gains needs to understand the
reality of momentum.

— *Napoleon Hill*

❧

July 29

Unless you know what you want,
you can't ask for it.

— *Jeanne Segal, Ph.D.*

In the life of every woman or any organization,
there are times when an added power is needed
to carry on through seeming failure to the point
of victory.

— *Napoleon Hill*

July 30

Always have some project underway . . .
an ongoing project that goes over from day to
day and thus makes each day a small
unit of time.

— Dr. Lillian Troll

Great physical power can be produced by
coordination of efforts but the endurance of
that power—its quality, scope, and strength are
taken from that intangible something known as
the "spirit" in which people work together for
the attainment of a common goal.

— Napoleon Hill

July 31

It is not fair to ask of others what you are not
willing to do yourself.

— Eleanor Roosevelt

It's a wise woman who understands that
there is strength in numbers and integrity
through unity.

— Napoleon Hill

Self-Discipline

Self-Discipline means taking possession of your own mind. Self-Discipline begins with the mastery of thought. If you do not control your thoughts, you cannot control your needs. Self-Discipline calls for a balancing of the emotions of your heart with the reasoning faculty of your head. It is the bottleneck through which all of your personal power for success must flow. Direct your thoughts, control your emotions, and ordain your destiny. As our culture has become more complex, the need for self-control has increased.

I can never lose sight of what it is that I want to pursue if I always take possession of my own reasoning and thoughts.

— *Wilma Jackson*

August 1

As tools become rusty, so does the mind; a
garden uncared for soon becomes smothered in
weeds; a talent neglected withers and dies.

— *Ethel R. Page*

People who keep on winning in life are those
who are willing to pay the price of success
in terms of developing and maintaining
constructive, success-producing habits.

— *Napoleon Hill*

August 2

We are always afraid to start something that we
want to make very good, true, and serious.

— *Brenda Ueland*

Self-discipline means taking possession of your
own mind.

— *Napoleon Hill*

August 3

I believe in hard work. It keeps the wrinkles out
of the mind and the spirit.

— *Helena Rubinstein*

What you are as a person, whether it be success
or failure, depends to a large degree upon your
personal habits.

— *Napoleon Hill*

August 4

Self-restraint may be alien to the human
temperament, but humanity without restraint
will dig its own grave.

— *Marya Mannes*

You can choose to create within you habits that
are success-producing.

— *Napoleon Hill*

August 5

There are two ways to meet difficulties.
You alter the difficulties or you alter
yourself to meet them.

— *Phyliss Bottome*

The most important habits are those which have
to do with the thoughts you think.

— *Napoleon Hill*

August 6

You have to learn the rules of the game.
And then, you have to play better than
anyone else.

— *Dianne Feinstein*

It doesn't take too long to realize that what
a woman thinks is translated into
physical terms with regard to what she
does and achieves in life.

— *Napoleon Hill*

AUGUST 7

In the end, we are all the sum total of our actions.
Character cannot be counterfeited, nor can it
be put on and cast off as if it were a garment to
meet the whim of the moment. Like the markings
on wood which are ingrained in the very heart
of the tree, character requires time and nurture
for growth and development. Thus also, day by
day, we write our own destiny; for inexorably
we become what we do. This I believe, is the
supreme logic and the law of life.

— *Madame Chiang Kai-shek*

When you have gained control over your
thought habits, you will have come a long way
in realizing the type of Self-Discipline that
speeds up the success process.

— *Napoleon Hill*

AUGUST 8

He who angers you, conquers you.

— *Elizabeth Kenny*

As a rule of thumb, keep your plans
to yourself.

— *Napoleon Hill*

August 9

What really matters is what you do with
what you have.

— *Shirley Lord*

Shoot for the stars! It may not be in the best
taste for you to over-shoot your abilities in
terms of personal ambition, but it is a lot better
than setting an easily obtainable goal which
requires little effort.

— *Napoleon Hill*

August 10

No one can avoid aging, but aging productively
is something else.

— *Katharine Graham*

If you aim at a very big achievement and only
obtain a moderate achievement, you still have
realized a goal of great value.

— *Napoleon Hill*

August 11

And remember this: if you think you're
too small to be effective—you've never been in
bed with a mosquito.

— *Anita Roddick*

If you allow yourself to be held back in
the beginning, you will have only sold
yourself short.

— *Napoleon Hill*

August 12

All serious daring starts from within.

— *Eudora Welty*

Self-discipline represents the "bottleneck"
through which the great power within this
Science must pass.

— *Napoleon Hill*

August 13

Challenges make you discover things about yourself that you never really knew. They're what make the instrument stretch—what makes you go beyond the norm.

— *Cicely Tyson*

Self-discipline is a quality/habit you should persistently apply as it grows stronger with the passing of time and moves you ever closer to success.

— *Napoleon Hill*

August 14

Even though you may want to move forward in your life, you may have one foot on the brakes. In order to be free, we must learn how to let go.

— *Mary Manin Morrissey*

Adopt the motto: "Deeds not words." Let your actions talk for you.

— *Napoleon Hill*

AUGUST 15

When people keep telling you that you can't do
a thing, you kind of like to try it.

— *Margaret Chase*

You will find a lot more people willing to
tear you down by discouragement than you
will find flattering you and building up your
ego. Of course, the best way to avoid such
discouragement is to confide in no one but
those who have a genuine sympathy with
your cause and an understanding of life's
great possibilities.

— *Napoleon Hill*

Learning from Adversity and Defeat

Every adversity carries with it the seed of an equivalent or greater benefit. Individual success usually is in exact proportion to the scope of the defeat the individual has experienced and mastered. Most so-called failures represent only a temporary defeat that may prove to be a blessing in disguise. Defeat is never the same as failure unless and until it has been accepted as such.

Isn't it interesting how your life, and all you have planned for, can change in an instant?

— *Betsy Carlson*

August 16

If we had no winter, the spring would not be
so pleasant; if we did not sometimes taste of
adversity, prosperity would not be
so welcome.

— *Anne Bradstreet*

Every adversity carries with it the seed of an
equivalent or a greater benefit provided
you look for it.

— *Napoleon Hill*

August 17

Mistakes are a fact of life. It is the response
to error that counts.

— *Nikki Giovanni*

Most so-called failures only represent
temporary setbacks which can prove to
be blessings in disguise.

— *Napoleon Hill*

AUGUST 18

Between two evils, I always pick the one I
never tried before.

— *Mae West*

Women who learn from adversity discover the
great pearls of the good life.

— *Napoleon Hill*

❦

AUGUST 19

The Slave knows that life is in
essence unpredictable.

— *Rebecca West*

Keep in mind that defeat is but a temporary
state of affairs unless you choose to accept
it as final.

— *Napoleon Hill*

AUGUST 20

Don't compromise yourself. You're all
you got.

— Janis Joplin

If we examine the records, we shall be
convinced that those women who attain success
are those who have adopted the habit of
accepting defeat as nothing but
an urge to greater effort.

— Napoleon Hill

AUGUST 21

I'm not afraid of storms for I'm learning
how to sail my ship.

— Louisa May Alcott

Time eventually corrects all evils, rights all
wrongs for those who realize that adversity is
one of the great teachers of life.

— Napoleon Hill

AUGUST 22

I have never been one who thought that the
Lord should make life easy; I've just asked Him
to make me strong.

— Eva Bowring

Defeat may lead to the development of a
stronger will-power, provided one accepts it as a
challenge to greater effort and not as a signal to
stop trying.

— Napoleon Hill

AUGUST 23

You may have a fresh start any moment you
choose, for this thing that we call "failure" is
not the falling down, but the staying down.

— Mary Pickford

Defeat may cause one to acquire the habit
of taking self-inventory for the purpose of
uncovering weaknesses responsible for
the defeat.

— Napoleon Hill

AUGUST 24

Reality is something you rise above.

— Liza Minnelli

Learning from adversity is a part of the great
system of natural laws designed by an all-wise
Creator to protect woman against her own
follies, save her from her own mistakes, and
insure her against self-destruction.

— Napoleon Hill

AUGUST 25

No soul that aspires can ever fail to rise;
no heart that loves can ever be abandoned.
Difficulties exist only that in overcoming them
we may grow strong.

— Annie Besant

Coming to grips with this principle could
produce a critical turning point in your life.

— Napoleon Hill

AUGUST 26

I'll say this for adversity: people seem to be
able to stand it, and that's more than I can say
for prosperity.

> — *Kim Hubbard*

The woman who "fails and still fights" usually
has uncovered a source of Creative Vision
enabling her to convert temporary defeat
into permanent success.

> — *Napoleon Hill*

AUGUST 27

People fail forward to success.

> — *Mary Kay Ash*

We shall find that the individual success usually
is in exact proportion to the scope of the defeat
the individual has experienced and mastered.

> — *Napoleon Hill*

AUGUST 28

The greatest mistake you can make in life is to
be continually fearing that you will
make one.

— *Ellen Hubbard*

Often defeat breaks up some negative habits
one has formed, thus releasing energies for a
new start through the development of more
positive habits.

— *Napoleon Hill*

AUGUST 29

. . . Most turning points are evident only
afterward, when the fact that had to have
been there is revealed.

— *Amanda Cross*

The compensating benefits of failure and defeat
often cannot be seen or recognized
as benefits until one looks backward at the
experiences after a sufficient lapse of time.

— *Napoleon Hill*

AUGUST 30

Don't fight the waves. Dive under, bob up, or
catch the curl and ride the wave. The ocean
is stronger than you: you might as well be a
matchstick in comparison. But if you yield to the
waves, they carry you, their power becomes you.
— *Elizabeth Cunningham*

The person who can go through defeat
which crushes the finer emotions, and still
avoid having her inner soul smothered by the
experience may become a master in her
chosen field of endeavor.
— *Napoleon Hill*

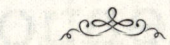

AUGUST 31

When you get into a tight place and everything
goes against you, 'til it seems as though you
could not hold on a minute longer, never give
up then, for that is just the place and time that
the tide will turn.
— *Harriet Beecher Stowe*

It is crucial to note that the turning point
at which one begins to attain success in
the higher brackets of achievement usually
is marked by some form of outstanding
defeat or failure.
— *Napoleon Hill*

Controlled Attention

Controlled Attention leads to mastery in any type of human endeavor, because it enables one to focus the powers of his mind upon the attainment of a definite objective and to keep it so directed at will. Great achievements come from minds that are at peace with themselves. Peace within one's mind is not a matter of luck, but is a priceless possession, which can be attained only by Self-Discipline based upon Controlled Attention. Concentration on one's major purpose projects a clear picture of that purpose upon the conscious mind and holds it there until it is taken over by the subconscious mind and acted upon.

I enjoy being challenged, and I strive to seek out the impossible in order to prove that <u>impossible</u> becomes the <u>possible</u> when I enter the situation with a focused mind and a clear vision of the purpose.

— *Carol Macinga*

September 1

Only when I make room for the child's voice
within me do I feel genuine and creative.

— *Alice Miller*

The mind never remains inactive. It works
continuously, reacting to those influences which
reach it.

— *Napoleon Hill*

September 2

Listening creates holy silence. Listening
is like the rain.

— *Rachel Naomi Remen*

Controlled Attention is an absolute prerequisite
if one is to tap into the great reservoir of power
with Infinite Intelligence.

— *Napoleon Hill*

September 3

We ought to be able to learn some things
secondhand. There is not enough time for us to
make all the mistakes ourselves.

— Harriet Hall

Controlled Attention is the highest form
of Self-Discipline.

— Napoleon Hill

September 4

Power is the ability to do good things
for others.

— Brooke Astor

Great achievements come from minds which
are at peace with themselves and to those who
are at peace with others.

— Napoleon Hill

SEPTEMBER 5

Old fashioned ways which no longer apply to
changed conditions are a snare in which the
feet of women have always become
readily entangled.

— *Jane Addams*

The difference between Controlled Attention
and casual attention is very great. It amounts to a
difference between feeding the mind on thought
material which will produce that which one
desires, and allowing the mind through neglect to
feed upon the type of garbage that will produce
that which one most fears and least desires.

— *Napoleon Hill*

SEPTEMBER 6

You need to claim the events of your life to
make yourself yours. When you truly possess all
that you have been and done, which may take
some time, you are fierce with reality.

— *Florida Scott-Maxwell*

Controlled Attention, when it is focused upon
the object of one's Definite Major Purpose,
is the medium by which one makes positive
application of the principle and process of
autosuggestion.

— *Napoleon Hill*

SEPTEMBER 7

Risk! Risk anything! Care no more for the
opinions of others. Do the hardest thing on
earth for you. Act for yourself. Face the truth.

— *Katherine Mansfield*

Keep your mind on the things you want and off
the things you don't want.

— *Napoleon Hill*

SEPTEMBER 8

She had nothing to fall back on: not maleness,
not whiteness, not ladyhood, not anything. And
out of the profound desolation of her reality she
may well have invented herself.

— *Toni Morrison*

A good example is a person whose thoughts
are fixed upon failure and poverty. Through
autosuggestion such thoughts as "I'm a loser"
or "I'll never have anything" are transferred
to the subconscious mind, fed back into the
conscious mind and are expressed as actions
which guarantee that the person will lose and
have little in life.

— *Napoleon Hill*

SEPTEMBER 9

Show me how you follow your deepest desires,
spiraling down into the ache with the ache, and
I will show you how I reach inward and open
outward to feel the kiss of the Mystery, sweet
lips on my own, every day.

— *Oriah Mountain Dreamer*

It is obvious that when one voluntarily fixes her
attention upon a Definite Major Purpose of a
positive nature, and forces her mind to dwell on
that purpose, that she "conditions" her mind to
act upon that purpose.

— *Napoleon Hill*

ﮩﮩ৩ﮩﮩ

SEPTEMBER 10

There is no point at which you can say,
"Well, I am successful now. I might as
well take a nap."

— *Carrie Fisher*

Controlled Attention may be compared to a
gardener who keeps her fertile garden spot
cleared of weeds so that it may yield a bountiful
harvest of edible foods.

— *Napoleon Hill*

SEPTEMBER 11

Maybe being oneself is always an
acquired taste.

— *Patricia Hampl*

Controlled Attention is self-mastery of the
highest order. It reflects organized
mind-power. Actually, Controlled Attention and
Self-Discipline are so closely related that they
can be best described as "twin brothers."

— *Napoleon Hill*

SEPTEMBER 12

No one is so eager to gain new experience as he
who doesn't know how to make use of the
old ones.

— *Marie Ebner von Eshenbach*

One either takes possession of her own mind
and directs it to the attainment of that which
she desires or her mind takes possession of her
and gives her whatever the circumstances of life
hand out.

— *Napoleon Hill*

SEPTEMBER 13

I must govern the clock, not be
governed by it.

— *Golda Meir*

Perhaps you can better understand how the
principle of Controlled Attention works if you
realize that one can control the span and object
of attention by thinking of it, talking of it, eating
it, drinking it, sleeping and dreaming it and thus
making it a twenty-four hour obsession.

— *Napoleon Hill*

SEPTEMBER 14

The funny thing about going after success in any
venture is that there is no failure as long as you
pay attention to your results.

— *Barrie Dolnick*

Controlled Attention is the act of focusing the
mind upon a given desire until the ways and
means for its realization have been worked out
and successfully put into operation.

— *Napoleon Hill*

SEPTEMBER 15

Thinkers rule the world. They always have
and they always will. All people think, but
the tragedy of life is that so few of us think
creatively or constructively; so few recognize the
fact that thought is a creative force.

— *Venice Bloodworth*

Success in all the higher brackets of individual
achievement is attained only by the application
of thought power, properly organized and
directed to definite ends.

— *Napoleon Hill*

Accurate Thinking

The power of thought is the most dangerous or the most beneficial power available to man, depending, of course, upon how it is used. Through the power of thought man builds great empires of civilization. Through the same power other people trample down empires as if they were helpless clay. Thought is the only thing over which man has been given the complete privilege of control. The Accurate Thinker always submits his emotional desires and decisions to his head for judiciary examination before he relies upon them as being sound, for he knows that his head is more dependable than his heart. The accurate thinker separates facts from fiction and separates facts into two classes: important and unimportant.

Accurate Thinking is a skill that will get you what you want. Many people get caught up in the action steps or the mechanics of how to go about getting something they want. In reality, the key to achieving a goal is your commitment and your intention.

— *Kathy Quinlan Perez*

September 16

The first problem for all of us, man and woman,
is not to learn, but to unlearn.

— *Gloria Steinem*

An accurate thinker sees both the way and
the doing of the way.

— *Napoleon Hill*

September 17

I'm not sure I want popular opinion on my
side—I've noticed those with the most opinions
often have the fewest facts.

— *Bethania McKenstry*

Accurate thinking is a grasping for conclusion
through intuition after all of the possibilities
within a given situation have been explored.

— *Napoleon Hill*

SEPTEMBER 18

Today, if you are not confused, you're just
not thinking clearly.

— *Irene Peter*

Remember, the accurate thinker is one who can
state a problem simply, clearly, and precisely.

— *Napoleon Hill*

SEPTEMBER 19

Action without study is fatal. Study without
action is futile.

— *Mary Beard*

Don't tackle a problem with a closed mind.

— *Napoleon Hill*

September 20

Think wrongly if you please, but in all cases think for yourself.

— *Doris Lessing*

The accurate thinker is always concerned that the decisions reached and applied are consistent with one's life goals or Definite Major Purpose.

— *Napoleon Hill*

September 21

The person who knows how will always have a job. The person who knows why will always be his boss.

— *Diane Ravitch*

Each decision you reach, each step you take, ought to draw you closer to realizing your Definite Major Purpose.

— *Napoleon Hill*

SEPTEMBER 22

Once you wake up thought in a man, you can
never put it to sleep again.

— Zora Neale Hurston

Be patient. Be courageous. You can find your
way out of the maze—a conclusion, a solution
awaits you as an accurate thinker.

— Napoleon Hill

SEPTEMBER 23

Expecting life to treat you well because you are
a good person is like expecting an angry bull not
to charge because you are a vegetarian.

— Shari R. Barr

There is no substitute for precise thinking.

— Napoleon Hill

SEPTEMBER 24

Let us be of good cheer, remembering that the
misfortunes hardest to bear are those
which never come.

— *Amy Lowell*

Stop trying to think out your problems alone
and begin using the knowledge and experience
and judgment of others.

— *Napoleon Hill*

SEPTEMBER 25

Never give up and never face the facts.

— *Ruth Gordon*

If the circumstances of your life are not to
your liking, you may change them by changing
your mental attitude to conform with the
circumstances you desire.

— *Napoleon Hill*

SEPTEMBER 26

The objective is not to pass, but to surpass.
— *Millie Thornton*

The habit of accurate, organized thinking pays off. There is no limit to the amount it pays when put into intelligent action, except the mental limitations which you set up in your own mind.
— *Napoleon Hill*

SEPTEMBER 27

Where I was born, and how I lived is unimportant. It is what I have done and where I have been that should be of interest.
— *Georgia O'Keeffe*

Next to life itself, the greatest miracle known to man is the miracle of thought, and no small part of this miracle consists in the amazing simplicity with which so complicated a mechanism as the brain can be operated by the power of will.
— *Napoleon Hill*

September 28

It is best to learn as we go, not go as we
have learned.

— Leslie Jeanne Sahler

There can be no fixed price on the value of
organized thinking! But there is no power in
thought until it is organized and directed toward a
definite end and implemented by intelligent action.

— Napoleon Hill

September 29

A closed mind is a dying mind.

— Edna Ferber

"The first fact one must recognize," said
Andrew Carnegie, "in order to become an
accurate thinker, is the fact that the power with
which one thinks is mental dynamite which
can be organized and used constructively for
the attainment of definite ends; but if not
controlled and directed, it may become a mental
explosive that will literally blast your hopes of
achievement and lead to inevitable failure."

— Napoleon Hill

SEPTEMBER 30

Well, maybe there is no profit on each individual
jar, but we'll make it up in volume.

— *Lucy Ricardo*

The person who can accurately think through
situations related to one's Definite Major
Purpose is a craftsman and rises quickly to
an enviable position.

— *Napoleon Hill*

Maintenance of Sound Health

The mind and the body are so closely related that whatever one does affects the other. One does not enjoy sound health without a health consciousness. Sound health begins with a sound health consciousness, just as financial success begins with a prosperity consciousness. To maintain a health consciousness, one must think in terms of sound health, not in terms of illness and disease. As the old sayings go: "You have nothing if you do not have your health" and "If you think you're sick, you are."

In order for us to remain healthy, both physically and emotionally, we must continue to stimulate ourselves with a healthy conscience and maintain a balance between body and mind.

— *Patsi Gately*

OCTOBER 1

Health is not a condition of matter, but of
mind, nor can the material senses bear reliable
testimony on the subject of health.

— *Mary Baker Eddy*

If you think you are sick, you are.

— *Napoleon Hill*

OCTOBER 2

Bodies never lie.

— *Agnes DeMille*

We cannot separate the body and the
mind, for they are one.

— *Napoleon Hill*

OCTOBER 3

We have no right to look for a happy old age if,
in our living, we habitually violate physical and
spiritual laws. The full blessing of length of days
comes to those who have known how to live, and
the beauty of the years of maturity can be assured
only by maintaining high standards of living.

— *Janet Baird*

A change in mental attitude often aids in
the development of bodily resistance
against disease.

— *Napoleon Hill*

OCTOBER 4

The more man follows nature and is
obedient to her laws, the longer he will
live; the further he deviates from these, the
shorter will be his existence. Health is nature's
reward for getting into harmony with her laws.

— *Anita Hesselgesser*

We are not only one in the sense of a mind-
body, but we are also part of the environment in
which we live.

— *Napoleon Hill*

OCTOBER 5

Humor is an excellent path to enlightenment.

— *Tama Stark*

The key to good health is a physically fit body
complemented by a Positive Mental Attitude
which is expressed as a positive
approach to life.

— *Napoleon Hill*

OCTOBER 6

There is a rainbow in you stronger than steel.

— *Megan Doherty*

Don't forget to express gratitude daily, by prayer
and affirmation, for the blessings you have.

— *Napoleon Hill*

OCTOBER 7

Fortunately, psychoanalysis is not the only way
to resolve inner conflicts. Life itself remains a
very effective therapist.

— Karen Horney

Success comes to those who are physically
and mentally fit.

— Napoleon Hill

OCTOBER 8

As I grow older, part of my emotional survival
plan must be to actively seek inspiration instead
of passively waiting for it to find me.

— Bebe Moore Campbell

Don't neglect to play and relax regularly.

— Napoleon Hill

OCTOBER 9

There is a fountain of youth: it is your mind,
your talents, the creativity you bring to your
life and the lives of people you love. When
you learn to tap this source, you will truly have
defeated age.

— *Sophia Loren*

Go to bed praying and get up singing and notice
what a fine day's work you will do.

— *Napoleon Hill*

OCTOBER 10

The biggest disease this day and age is that of
people feeling unloved.

— *Princess Diana*

Mental germs not only poison the psychological
system, but attack a person's
physical system as well.

— *Napoleon Hill*

OCTOBER 11

Raising your awareness of the relationship
between food and health is always a good
starting point for improving the quality of
your life.

— Barbara Berger

Eat right, think right, sleep right, and play right,
and you can save the doctor's bill for your
vacation money.

— Napoleon Hill

OCTOBER 12

The cure for anything is salt water—
sweat, tears, or the sea.

— Isak Dinesen

Don't try to cure a headache. It's better to cure
the thing that caused it.

— Napoleon Hill

OCTOBER 13

Guidance and support are there for those who
have the eyes to see, the ears to hear, and the
heart to accept what the Universe has to offer.

— *Sonia Choquette*

As we are one with the world about us, so are
we one with ourselves: a mind-body. And as we
are affected by the world we live in, and in turn
affect that world, so our body influences our
mind, and in turn our mind influences
our body.

— *Napoleon Hill*

OCTOBER 14

Women need real moments of solitude and self-
reflection to balance out how much of ourselves
we give away.

— *Barbara De Angelis*

The most successful person uses autosuggestion
as a medium for feeding her mind with the
thoughts of things and circumstances she
desires, including a health consciousness.

— *Napoleon Hill*

OCTOBER 15

Never go to a doctor whose office plants
have died.

— *Erma Bombeck*

Some live to eat, others eat to live, and they live
better and longer.

— *Napoleon Hill*

Budgeting
Time and Money

People are divided into two classes: drifters and non-drifters. A non-drifter is a person who has a definite major purpose, a definite plan to attain that purpose, and is busily engaged in carrying out his plan. A drifter does no real thinking. He acts upon the thinking of others. Successful people ask themselves the following questions:

- How are you using your time?
- How much of it are you wasting, and
- How are you wasting it?
- What are you doing to stop this waste?
- Tell me how you use your spare time and how you spend your money, and I will tell you where and what you will be ten years from now.

It is easy to say 'no' when you understand what you desire.

— *Phyllis Baker*

OCTOBER 16

We say we waste time, but that is impossible.
We waste ourselves.

— Alice Bloch

Yesterday is gone forever, now make the most
of today and tomorrow if you wish to
make up for lost time.

— Napoleon Hill

OCTOBER 17

Imagine waking up every morning and
discovering a list of all the things that make you
great. Well, don't just imagine it . . . do it!

— Nancy E. Krulik

Every woman needs to stop, look, listen and
think. And she should do this with regularity,
with purpose aforethought. She should take
personal inventory of herself at least once a
month, to make sure that she is getting the most
out of life, or to find out why she is not.

— Napoleon Hill

OCTOBER 18

I've been on a calendar, but never on time.

— *Marilyn Monroe*

Remember also that you will never be ready to
receive the better things of life which you desire
unless you put yourself under a strict system of
self-discipline in the use of your time.

— *Napoleon Hill*

OCTOBER 19

Change your mind about money today and
change your experience with money tomorrow.
Try it and see.

— *Chellie Campbell*

Every woman is where she is, and what she
is, because of the habits she has acquired. The
woman who lives up to the limit of her income,
or beyond it, never is a free woman.

— *Napoleon Hill*

OCTOBER 20

Just about the time you think you can make
both ends meet, somebody moves the ends.

— *Pansy Penner*

Frugality is one of the essentials of success. The
habit of planned savings encourages frugality,
makes it an established habit.

— *Napoleon Hill*

❧

OCTOBER 21

When I'm about to take a risk, I consider the
down side. If it's not death, I do it.

— *Nancy Sardella*

Self-examination requires self-discipline,
courage, sincerity and a willingness to face facts.
Successful women always are their own most
severe critics and taskmasters. They maneuver
the circumstances of their lives to their own
advantage, instead of procrastinating and allowing
circumstances to maneuver them into failure.

— *Napoleon Hill*

OCTOBER 22

What you love is as unique to you as your
fingerprints. You need to know that because
nothing will make you really happy but doing
what you love.

— Barbara Sher

The happiest women are those who have
learned to mix play with their work and bind the
two together with enthusiasm.

— Napoleon Hill

OCTOBER 23

I've been rich and I've been poor.
Rich is better.

— Sophie Tucker

The major purpose of a budget system is
to establish habits which force one to save
a definite percentage of her income so that
eventually she may acquire economic
independence.

— Napoleon Hill

OCTOBER 24

If you want more, pay more.

— Stella Adler

Readiness calls for preparation through the
conditioning of your mind to accept
guidance from within.

— Napoleon Hill

OCTOBER 25

Self-respect is a question of recognizing that
anything worth having has its price.

— Joan Didion

The Creator gave you a brain to be used and
constant access to the power of thought which
flows into your brain from the great storehouse
of Infinite Intelligence. What use are you
making of this power?

— Napoleon Hill

OCTOBER 26

Money is like manure—it's not worth anything
unless you spread it around.

> — *Dolly Levi*

Use your time wisely. Invest it in creating
relationships which are mutually rewarding
and harmonious.

> — *Napoleon Hill*

OCTOBER 27

Yesterday is a canceled check, tomorrow is a
promissory note, today is ready cash—use it.

> — *Kay Lyons*

If you wish a job done promptly and well, get a
busy woman to do it.

> — *Napoleon Hill*

OCTOBER 28

All shall be well
and all shall be well
and all manner of thing shall be well.

— Julian of Norwich

Clear your mind of all anxieties, all desires, all
fears, and give your Creator an opportunity to
speak to you.

— Napoleon Hill

OCTOBER 29

There is no pleasure in having nothing to do;
the fun is in having lots to do and not doing it.

— Mary Wilson Little

Yes, your real boss is the person who walks
around under your hat. Recognize this truth and
you will have an adequate incentive to use your
time effectively.

— Napoleon Hill

OCTOBER 30

It is the simple things of life that make living
worthwhile, the sweet fundamental things such
as love and duty, work and rest, and living close
to nature.

— Laura Ingalls Wilder

By freeing your mind for one hour each day you
will be inviting opportunity to reveal itself
to you.

— Napoleon Hill

OCTOBER 31

A woman's best protection is a little money
of her own.

— Clare Booth Luce

Make your money work for you and you will not
have to work so hard for it.

— Napoleon Hill

Creative
Vision

Creative Vision is developed by the free
and fearless use of one's imagination. Creative
Vision attains its ends by basically new ideas
and methods. It is not a miraculous quality with
which one is gifted or is not gifted at birth. It is
a quality that may be developed. It may be an
inborn quality of mind, or an acquired quality,
for it may be developed by the free and fearless
use of the faculty of imagination. Our country
needs Creative Vision now as it has never
needed it before.

By imagining something first, I was able to
actually make the vision become a reality.

— *Thelzeda Moore*

NOVEMBER 1

The next time your mind wanders,
follow it around for awhile.

— *Jessica Masterson*

Creative Vision is the capacity to envision new
possibilities, dream new dreams, and tap into
the vast powers of the universe which permit
you to build a new tomorrow as you achieve
your Definite Major Purpose.

— *Napoleon Hill*

NOVEMBER 2

When you obey all the rules, you miss all
the fun.

— *Katherine Hepburn*

Creative Vision is much more than simply a
game of "let's try and think of a new idea."

— *Napoleon Hill*

NOVEMBER 3

Memory feeds imagination.

— Amy Tan

A woman introspects, which means she is
capable of "tuning" in to her inner self.

— Napoleon Hill

NOVEMBER 4

Before you can do something that you've never
done before, you have to be able to imagine
it's possible.

— Jean Shinoda Bolen

Imagination is the key to all achievement, the
mainspring of all human endeavor, and the
secret door leading to the inner-woman.

— Napoleon Hill

NOVEMBER 5

It is the creative potential itself in human beings
that is the image of God.

— Mary Daly

Creative Vision is more tuned to the creative
spirit of the universe which expresses itself
through woman.

— Napoleon Hill

NOVEMBER 6

Imagination is the highest kite one can fly.

— Lauren Bacall

Creative Vision is reserved for the
sensitive, inspired, open-ended person who
enjoys life and wishes to drink from its
deepest wells.

— Napoleon Hill

NOVEMBER 7

Today is the full bloom of life. The petals of
yesterday have shriveled in the past. Tomorrow
is an unopened bud that may be blackened by
the frost or beautified by the sun of life.

— *Coletta Davidson*

Imagination is the soil within which flowers
the creative effort distinguishing
winners from losers.

— *Napoleon Hill*

NOVEMBER 8

Each one of us is God's special work of art.
Through us, He teaches and inspires . . . those
who view our lives.

— *Joni Eareckson Tada*

Creative Vision is definitely related to that
state of mind known as Faith, and it is deeply
significant that those who have demonstrated
the greatest amount of creative vision are
known to have been women with a great
capacity for faith.

— *Napoleon Hill*

November 9

Every thought we think is creating our future.

— *Louise L. Hay*

Creative Vision is not a miraculous quality with
which one is gifted or not gifted at birth.

— *Napoleon Hill*

November 10

Sometimes the only way to tell if there's an open
door is to try to step through it.

— *Heidi S. Hess*

Creative Vision is a quality which may
be developed.

— *Napoleon Hill*

NOVEMBER 11

Defining myself, as opposed to being defined by
others, is one of the most difficult challenges
I face.

— *Carol Moseley-Braun*

Creative Vision assists you in discovering who
you are, what you want from life, and what you
are willing to give in return.

— *Napoleon Hill*

NOVEMBER 12

Creativity is . . . seeing something that doesn't
exist already. You need to find out how you can
bring it into being and that way be a playmate
with God.

—*Michele Shea*

The dare to do spirit of Creative Vision inspires
women to pioneer and experiment in every field
of endeavor.

— *Napoleon Hill*

November 13

The most lethal weapon in the world's arsenal is
not the neutron bomb or chemical warfare but
the human mind that devises such things and
puts them to use.

— Margaret Atwood

Our country needs Creative Vision now as it has
never needed it before.

— Napoleon Hill

November 14

The world is wide, and I will not waste my life
in friction when it could be turned
into momentum.

— Frances Willard

Our nation has plenty of brawn and muscle—
but what is needed desperately is an outpouring
of Creative Vision if we are to meet the very
complex demands we now face and surmount
the crisis of complex international relationships
upon which the peace and prosperity of the
world depends.

— Napoleon Hill

NOVEMBER 15

For each of us as women, there is a deep place
within, where hidden and growing our true spirit
rises. . . . Within these deep places, each one holds
an incredible reserve of creativity and power, of
unexamined and unrecorded emotion and feeling.

— *Audre Lorde*

Adopt the habit of the "silent hour" when you
will be still and listen for that small, still voice
that speaks from within, thus discovering the
greatest of all power, Creative Vision, the great
power that can help you achieve your Definite
Major Purpose.

— *Napoleon Hill*

NOVEMBER 16

Woman, if the soul of the nation is to be saved,
I believe that you must become its soul.

— *Coretta Scott King*

The woman possessing Creative Vision knows
that she succeeds only by helping others to
succeed, and she knows that it is not necessary
for another woman to fail in order that she
may succeed.

— *Napoleon Hill*

NOVEMBER 17

To gain what is worth having, it may be
necessary to lose everything else.

— Bernadette Devlin

A woman with Creative Vision knows what she
desires of life and understands that life never
permits anyone to get something of value for
nothing without eventually having to pay more
for it than it is worth.

— Napoleon Hill

NOVEMBER 18

Believe in something larger than yourself . . .
Get involved in some of the big ideas of
your time.

— Barbara Bush

Creative Vision is a quality of mind belonging
only to women who follow the habit of
Going the Extra Mile. It recognizes no such
thing as the regularity of working hours and
it is not primarily concerned with monetary
compensation as its highest aim is to achieve
the "impossible."

— Napoleon Hill

NOVEMBER 19

I think the key is for women not to set
any limits.

— Martina Navratilova

The woman with Creative Vision knows
where she is going.

— Napoleon Hill

NOVEMBER 20

We would like to believe that we are not in the
business of surviving but in being good, and
we do not like to admit to ourselves that we are
good in order to survive.

— Dorothy Rowe

The woman with Creative Vision has no fear
of others, either those of higher or lower rank,
for she is at peace with herself and is fair and
honest in her relationships with others
and herself.

— Napoleon Hill

NOVEMBER 21

I soon realized that no journey carries one far
unless, as it extends into the world around us, it
goes an equal distance into the world within.

— *Lillian Smith*

You must go into the silence alone of your own
free will and accord.

— *Napoleon Hill*

NOVEMBER 22

Energy creates energy. It is by spending oneself
that one becomes rich.

— *Sarah Bernhardt*

The woman with Creative Vision produces
results, not excuses.

— *Napoleon Hill*

NOVEMBER 23

Don't be afraid of the space between your
dreams and reality. If you can dream it,
you can make it so.

— *Belva Davis*

Developing Creative Vision keeps a woman so
busy achieving her Definite Major Purpose that
there is not time left for worry and doubt or fear
and frustration.

— *Napoleon Hill*

NOVEMBER 24

I realized that if what we call human nature can
be changed, then absolutely anything is possible.
And from that moment, my life changed.

— *Shirley MacLaine*

It is a well-known fact that any idea, plan or
purpose, that is brought into the conscious
mind repeatedly and supported by the
emotional feeling is automatically picked up
by the subconscious section of the mind and
carried out to its logical conclusion by means of
whatever practical media are at hand.

— *Napoleon Hill*

November 25

As we become purer channels for God's light,
we develop an appetite for the sweetness that is
possible in this world. A miracle worker is not
geared toward fighting the world that is, but
toward creating the world that could be.

—*Marianne Williamson*

The imagination has been described as "the
workshop of the soul wherein is shaped all plans
for individual achievement."

— *Napoleon Hill*

November 26

But this freedom is only the beginning; the
room is your own, but it is still bare. It
has to be furnished; it has to be decorated;
it has to be shared. How are you going to
furnish it, how are you going to decorate it?
With whom are you going to share it, and upon
what terms?

— *Virginia Woolf*

Locked deep within the human spirit is a vast
reservoir of ideas and insights waiting to
be released.

— *Napoleon Hill*

NOVEMBER 27

The cure for boredom is curiosity.
There is no cure for curiosity.

— Ellen Parr

Nearly every fact or idea known to man is but
a combination of older realities rearranged to
create a new appearance or synthesis. This is
synthetic imagination.

— Napoleon Hill

NOVEMBER 28

The only thing that makes life possible is
permanent, intolerable uncertainty;
not knowing what comes next.

— Ursula K. LeGuin

The other type of imagination is Creative
Imagination which has its base in the
subconscious section of the mind and serves
as the medium by which new facts or ideas are
revealed through the faculty known as the
"sixth sense."

— Napoleon Hill

NOVEMBER 29

"But it is always interesting when one doesn't
see," she added. "If you don't see what a thing
means, you must be looking at it wrong
way around."

— *Agatha Christie*

The soil within which great creative efforts
blossom can be enriched by applying the
seventeen success principles; i.e., the Science
of Success.

— *Napoleon Hill*

NOVEMBER 30

People are like stained glass windows— the true
beauty can be seen only when there is light from
within. The darker the night, the brighter
the windows.

— *Elisabeth Kübler-Ross*

The point can be made—"It makes little
difference where a woman begins."

— *Napoleon Hill*

Cosmic Habitforce

Cosmic Habitforce pertains to the universe
as a whole and the laws that govern it. Cosmic
Habitforce is Infinite Intelligence in operation.
It is a sense of order. It takes over a habit
and causes a person to act upon the habit
automatically. Developing and establishing
positive habits leads to peace of mind, health,
and financial security. You are where you are
and what you are because of your established
habits and thoughts and deeds.

I tell others that first you get a good habit
and then it will carry you to wherever you
want to go.

— *Yang Ping*

December 1

Where thou art, that is Home.

— *Emily Dickinson*

The orderliness of the world gives evidence that
all natural laws are under the control
of a universal plan.

— *Napoleon Hill*

⚜

December 2

Hurt No Living Thing
Hurt no living thing;
Ladybird, nor butterfly,
Nor moth with dusty wing,
Nor cricket chirping cheerily,
Nor grasshopper so light of leap,
Nor dancing gnat, not beetle fat,
Nor harmless worms that creep.

— *Christina Rossetti*

Cosmic Habitforce pertains to the entire
universe and is the law by which the equilibrium
of the universe is maintained through
established patterns or habits.

— *Napoleon Hill*

DECEMBER 3

I share Einstein's affirmation that anyone who
is not lost on the rapturous awe at the power
and glory of the mind behind the universe "is as
good as a burnt out candle."

— Madeleine L'Engle

Cosmic Habitforce is Infinite Intelligence
in action.

— Napoleon Hill

DECEMBER 4

Here's the good news: God is a nag. God won't
give up. If we are destined to carry out some
divine idea, we won't be able to shrug it off.
For me, God doesn't just whisper within. If I'm
supposed to get a message, I start to see it and
hear it everywhere—books, sermons, television
shows, conversations with friends.

— Ellen Debenport

Be sure to make your plan sufficiently flexible
so that you can change it any time that you are
inspired to do so . . . Infinite Intelligence may
hand you a better plan than the one you have
made for yourself for the achievement of
your purpose.

— Napoleon Hill

December 5

We all have the extraordinary coded within us
waiting to be released.

— *Jean Houston*

Nothing is ever produced which does not bear
many, or all, of the characteristics of
its ancestors.

— *Napoleon Hill*

December 6

The horizon leans forward, offering you space
to place new steps of change.

— *Maya Angelou*

If you treat hunches as foolish ideas, they will
soon treat you the same way and stay away.
When you have a hunch, no matter how foolish
it may seem, put it down on paper. Examine
it carefully, and you may find that it may be
an assist from Infinite Intelligence intended to
put you back on the beam, when you may have
gotten off.

— *Napoleon Hill*

DECEMBER 7

Today I know that I cannot control the ocean
tides. I can only go with the flow.

— *Marie Stilkind*

Cosmic Habitforce is the law which forces every
living creature, and every particle of matter,
to come under the dominating influence of its
environment, including the physical habits and
thought habits of mankind.

— *Napoleon Hill*

DECEMBER 8

Nature does not ask permission. Blossom and
birth whenever you feel like it.

— *Clarissa Pinkola Estes*

Control your mental attitude, keep it positive
by exercising self-discipline, and thus prepare
the mental soil in which any worthwhile plan,
purpose or desire may be planted by repeated,
intense impression, with the assurance that
it will germinate, grow and find expression
ultimately in its material equivalent, through
whatever means are at hand.

— *Napoleon Hill*

December 9

Whether we are poets or parents or teachers or
artists or gardeners, we must start where we are
and use what we have . . .
What seems mundane and trivial may show
itself to be holy, precious, part of a pattern.

— *Luci Shaw*

Nature and the universe are organized and
ordered. This order, or reliability, of
nature simplifies life.

— *Napoleon Hill*

December 10

Originality is not doing something no one else
has ever done, but doing what has been done
countless times with new life,
new breath.

— *Marie Chapian*

Time, space, energy, matter and intelligence are
nature's building blocks with which she creates
all things.

— *Napoleon Hill*

DECEMBER 11

In the end, what affects your life most deeply
are things too simple to talk about.

— *Nell Blaine*

An oak tree grows from an acorn, and a pine
tree grows from a pine nut. An acorn never
produces a pine tree, nor does a pine nut
produce an oak tree. Nothing is ever produced
which does not bear many, or all,
of the characteristics of its ancestors.

— *Napoleon Hill*

DECEMBER 12

Success doesn't come to you, you go get it.

— *Marva Collins*

There is nothing that is not controlled by this
universal law of Cosmic Habitforce.

— *Napoleon Hill*

December 13

Waiting until everything is perfect before
making a move is like waiting to start a trip until
all the traffic lights are green.

— *Karen Ireland*

Negative thought habits attract to their creator
physical manifestations corresponding to their
nature as perfectly and as inevitably as nature
germinates the acorn and develops it into an
oak tree.

— *Napoleon Hill*

December 14

We need to approach our state of mind with
curiosity and open wonder. That curious
listening to life is a joy—no matter what the
mood of our life is.

—*Charlotte Joko Beck*

As we have seen, our thought habits,
our mental attitude, are the one and only
things over which each individual has the
right of complete control.

— *Napoleon Hill*

DECEMBER 15

There is only one path to Heaven.
On Earth, we call it Love.

— *Karen Goldman*

All voluntary positive habits are the products
of will power directed toward the attainment of
definite goals.

— *Napoleon Hill*

DECEMBER 16

Remember that you are all people and that all
people are you. Remember that you are this
universe and that this universe is you.

— *Joy Harjo*

Women are all born equal in the sense that they
have equal access to this great principle. All
normal persons have the right to control their
thoughts and their mental attitude, and this is
the way in which this greatest of all natural laws
is made effective in individual lives.

— *Napoleon Hill*

December 17

We stand now where two roads diverge. But
unlike the roads in Robert Frost's familiar poem,
they are not equally fair. The road we have long
been traveling is deceptively easy, a smooth
superhighway on which we progress with great
speed, but at its end lies disaster. The other fork
of the road—the "one less traveled by"—offers
our last, our only chance to reach a destination
that assures the preservation of the earth.

— Rachel Carson

All big things are composed of smaller things of
a related nature.

— Napoleon Hill

December 18

Never, never rest contented with any circle of
ideas, but always be certain that a
wider one is still possible.

— Pearl Bailey

osmic Habitforce has the capacity to impart a
uliar quality to one's habits of thought which
es obstacles and provides a power capable
ounting barriers to success.

— Napoleon Hill

December 19

Learn to practice.

— *Martha Graham*

Our habits are created through repeated
thought and experience.

— *Napoleon Hill*

December 20

Desire, ask, believe, receive.

— *Stella Terrill Mann*

Cosmic Habitforce is the comptroller of all
natural laws.

— *Napoleon Hill*

December 21

For visions come not to polluted eyes.

— *Mary Howitt*

It's a great moment in your life when you break
away from your social heredity and start doing
your own thinking.

— *Napoleon Hill*

December 22

The dream is real, my friends. The failure to
realize it is the only unreality.

— *Toni Cade Bambara*

If you allow the fear of criticism, doubt and
other people's negative suggestions to take
shape in your mind, it will blot out the picture
of your major purpose.

— *Napoleon Hill*

DECEMBER 23

We have been taught to believe that
negative equals realistic and positive
equals unrealistic.

— Susan Jeffers

The same law which holds our earth in its orbit
and relates it to all other planets in their orbits,
both in time and space, relates human beings to
one another in exact conformity with the nature
of their own thoughts.

— Napoleon Hill

DECEMBER 24

I've arrived at this outermost edge of my life
by my own actions. Where I am is thoroughly
unacceptable. Therefore, I must stop doing
what I've been doing.

— Alice Killer

When you speak of your ambitions, if at all,
use the past tense, after they have become
accomplishments and are not just words.

— Napoleon Hill

December 25

Whether you know it or not, fear has developed
your likes and dislikes, picked your friends, and
raised your children.

— *Rhonda Britten*

Mental habits as well, including both poverty
consciousness and prosperity consciousness, are
fixed through the law of Cosmic Habitforce.

— *Napoleon Hill*

December 26

I have a simple philosophy. Fill what's empty.
Empty what's full. And scratch where it itches.

— *Alice Roosevelt Longworth*

The stars and planets operate with clocklike
precision. They never collide, never get off their
appointed course, but roll on eternally, as the
result of a preconceived plan.

— *Napoleon Hill*

DECEMBER 27

To be able to be caught up into the world of thought—that is being educated.

— *Edith Hamilton*

Let us repeat once more, for the sake of emphasis: your mind acts like an electro-magnet to attract to you the things upon which you keep it focused.

— *Napoleon Hill*

DECEMBER 28

There never was night that had no morn.

— *Dinah Mulock Craik*

The major distinguishing characteristic of Cosmic Habitforce is that it forces all repeated actions to become fixed habits, whether these be the thoughts of a person or the orderly movement of the stars or the coming and going of the seasons.

— *Napoleon Hill*

DECEMBER 29

Some tension is necessary for the soul to grow,
and we can put that tension to good use. We
can look for every opportunity to give and
receive love, to appreciate nature, to heal our
wounds and the wounds of others, to forgive
and to serve.

— Joan Borysenko

A strong will does not dwell on the past. A vital
ego thrives on the hopes and desires of the yet
unattained objective.

— Napoleon Hill

DECEMBER 30

The game of life is a game of boomerangs. Our
thoughts, deeds and words return to us sooner
or later with astounding accuracy.

— Florence Scovel Shinn

You are where you are and what you are
because of your established habits of
thoughts and deeds.

— Napoleon Hill

DECEMBER 31

Put your ear down close to your soul and
listen hard.

— Anne Sexton

You now understand why the greatest of all
riches is a Positive Mental Attitude, for by
means of such an attitude it is possible to
acquire all other things which you may
rightfully desire and possess.
What the mind can conceive and believe,
it can achieve with PMA!

— Napoleon Hill

NOTES

NOTES

NOTES